Obesity

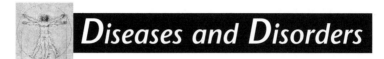

Diseases and Disorders

Obesity

Titles in the Diseases and Disorders series include:

Acne
Alzheimer's Disease
Anorexia and Bulimia
Anthrax
Arthritis
Asthma
Attention Deficit Disorder
Autism
Breast Cancer
Cerebral Palsy
Chronic Fatigue Syndrome
Cystic Fibrosis
Diabetes
Down Syndrome
Epilepsy
Headaches
Hemophilia
Hepatitis
Learning Disabilities
Leukemia
Lyme Disease
Multiple Sclerosis
Phobias
SARS
Schizophrenia
Sexually Transmitted Diseases
Sleep Disorders
Smallpox
West Nile Virus

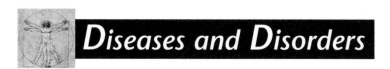

Diseases and Disorders

Obesity

Melissa Abramovitz

LUCENT
BOOKS®

THOMSON
———★——— ™
GALE

San Diego • Detroit • New York • San Francisco • Cleveland
New Haven, Conn. • Waterville, Maine • London • Munich

LIBRARY OF CONGRESS CATALOGING-IN-PUBLICATION DATA

Abramovitz, Melissa, 1954–
    Obesity / by Melissa Abramovitz.
        p. cm. — (Diseases and disorders)
    Summary: Examines the growing health problem of obesity, its social and emotional
impacts, causes, and treatment, and research that is being conducted, not only on new
drug therapies, diet, and exercise, but also on improved education.
    Includes bibliographical references and index.
    ISBN 1-59018-413-0 (hardback : alk. paper)
    1. Obesity—Juvenile literature. [1. Obesity.] I. Title. II. Diseases and disorders series.
    RC628.A25 2004
    616.3'98—dc22
                                                            2003020199

Printed in the United States of America

Table of Contents

"The Most Difficult Puzzles Ever Devised"

C HARLES BEST, ONE of the pioneers in the search for a cure for diabetes, once explained what it is about medical research that intrigued him so. "It's not just the gratification of knowing one is helping people," he confided, "although that probably is a more heroic and selfless motivation. Those feelings may enter in, but truly, what I find best is the feeling of going toe to toe with nature, of trying to solve the most difficult puzzles ever devised. The answers are there somewhere, those keys that will solve the puzzle and make the patient well. But how will those keys be found?"

Since the dawn of civilization, nothing has so puzzled people—and often frightened them, as well—as the onset of illness in a body or mind that had seemed healthy before. A seizure, the inability of a heart to pump, the sudden deterioration of muscle tone in a small child—being unable to reverse such conditions or even to understand why they occur was unspeakably frustrating to healers. Even before there were names for such conditions, even before they were understood at all, each was a reminder of how complex the human body was, and how vulnerable.

While our grappling with understanding diseases has been frustrating at times, it has also provided some of humankind's most heroic accomplishments. Alexander Fleming's accidental discovery in 1928 of a mold that could be turned into penicillin has resulted in the saving of untold millions of lives. The isolation of the enzyme insulin has reversed what was once a death sentence for anyone with diabetes. There have been great strides in combating conditions for which there is not yet a cure, too. Medicines can help AIDS patients live longer, diagnostic tools such as mammography and ultrasounds can help doctors find tumors while they are treatable, and laser surgery techniques have made the most intricate, minute operations routine.

This "toe-to-toe" competition with diseases and disorders is even more remarkable when seen in a historical continuum. An astonishing amount of progress has been made in a very short time. Just two hundred years ago, the existence of germs as a cause of some diseases was unknown. In fact, it was less than 150 years ago that a British surgeon named Joseph Lister had difficulty persuading his fellow doctors that washing their hands before delivering a baby might increase the chances of a healthy delivery (especially if they had just attended to a diseased patient)!

Each book in Lucent's Diseases and Disorders series explores a disease or disorder and the knowledge that has been accumulated (or discarded) by doctors through the years. Each book also examines the tools used for pinpointing a diagnosis, as well as the various means that are used to treat or cure a disease. Finally, new ideas are presented—techniques or medicines that may be on the horizon.

Frustration and disappointment are still part of medicine, for not every disease or condition can be cured or prevented. But the limitations of knowledge are being pushed outward constantly; the "most difficult puzzles ever devised" are finding challengers every day.

A Growing Health Problem

O BESITY HAS EXISTED throughout human history. Archaeologists have even uncovered statues depicting extremely obese people dating from prehistoric times. One of the oldest such statues discovered is known as the Venus of Willendorf. Found in the Austrian town of Willendorf in 1908, it dates back to about 22,000 B.C. and is of an extremely obese woman (although it is thought to represent fertility). Other ancient statues depicting obese people have been found in caves on the Mediterranean island of Malta dating back about five thousand years.

The ancient Egyptians frequently mentioned obesity in their papyrus writings on medical matters, and their temples had many statues of obese men and women. Historians say that the fact that statues of obese people were placed alongside statues of people with other illnesses shows that the Egyptians probably considered obesity to be a disease.

The Roman physician Galen in the first century described one very obese man named Nichomachus of Smyrna who was supposedly so heavy he could not move from his bed. Other Roman authors wrote of a Roman senator who was too heavy to walk unless two slaves carried his belly for him. The ancient Greek physician Hippocrates, known as the father of medicine, wrote about the fact that fat people were more prone to sudden death than were lean ones. He recommended a series of actions for losing weight, including eating a high-fat diet to make the person grow tired of fat, eating only once a day, sleeping on a hard bed, and walking naked for exercise. Modern doctors now know that none of these recommendations are effective methods of losing weight; a high-fat diet is more likely to make someone gain weight, eating only once a day is unhealthy, sleeping on a hard bed has nothing to do with weight loss or gain, and walking for exercise is just as healthy whether or not a person wears clothes.

In the Middle Ages, stories and pictures depicting obese people were quite common, and during the Renaissance, they became even more common. Obesity was also illustrated in paintings by many Renaissance artists. The renowned painter Peter Paul Rubens, for example, painted many obese women. During that era, many new foods and beverages, such as corn, potatoes, coffee, tea, and chocolate, became commonplace, helping to diminish the prevalent famines and providing more sustenance leading to weight gain for many individuals.

Many of the paintings of Renaissance artist Peter Paul Rubens, including this one of Marie de Médicis, queen of France, feature obese women.

Chester A. Arthur was one of several American presidents who today would be considered obese. In his day, Arthur was seen as healthy and robust.

Over the past few hundred years, there have also been many stories and other depictions of extremely obese individuals. One well-known obese man was Daniel Lambert of England, born in 1770. At five feet eleven inches tall, Lambert supposedly weighed 448 pounds by the time he was twenty-three years old. When he was featured in an exhibition in London in 1806, a special carriage was built to transport him to the event. By the time he died at age thirty-nine, he weighed 739 pounds. His body was 112 inches around and his legs 37 inches around.

In the nineteenth century, obesity became more prevalent, although most obese people did not weigh nearly what Lambert did. At that time, many people thought that a stout individual was prosperous and secure. U.S. presidents Zachary Taylor, Millard Fillmore, Ulysses S. Grant, and Chester A. Arthur were all obese and considered to be prosperous, trustworthy, upstanding people—in part because of their stature. Fat cheeks, stomach, and thighs also made them appear to be "healthy" in contrast to the many emaciated people who suffered from tuberculosis and other such devastating diseases prevalent at the time.

Obesity became even more common in the twentieth century as modern vehicles and tools took the physical labor out of many peoples' lives and food became more plentiful. There have been many examples of extreme obesity in modern times. John Brower Minnoch of Washington State was one of the heaviest people on record at about fourteen hundred pounds. When Minnoch had to be rushed to the hospital due to heart and respiratory failure, it took thirteen people to move him. Walter Hudson of New York was another well-known heavy man who made headlines when he became stuck in his bedroom doorway in 1987 and had to be rescued by emergency workers.

Although most obese persons in modern times do not achieve the notoriety accorded Minnoch and Hudson, their condition causes many problems for them, and their numbers are growing. According to the World Health Organization, there are now over 1.7 billion overweight and obese people throughout the world. "Contrary to conventional wisdom, the obesity epidemic is not restricted to industrialized societies; in developing countries, it is estimated that over 115 million people suffer from obesity-related problems."[1]

As more and more people are affected by and experience health problems related to obesity, more and more health experts and government officials have become concerned about the problem. Today there is much research being conducted, and programs are being put into place to try to reduce the magnitude of the epidemic and to prevent the obesity problem from becoming even more widespread.

Chapter 1

What Is Obesity?

MANY PEOPLE VIEW obesity as a weakness of character or lack of willpower that allows individuals to eat so much they gain tremendous amounts of weight. Recently, however, an increasing number of experts are viewing obesity as a disease that affects millions of people, including children and teens.

According to the American Obesity Association, "When there is too much body fat, the result is obesity. Obesity is not a sign of a person being out of control. It is a serious medical disease that affects over a quarter of adults in the United States, and about 14% of children and adolescents. It is the second leading cause of preventable death after smoking."[2]

The association points out that obesity fits all the medical definitions of a disease, those definitions being "an interruption, cessation, or disorder of a bodily function, organ, or system."[3] The disorder that characterizes obesity is an accumulation of excess fat and weight that occurs over time when a person takes in more calories than they expend. A calorie is a measure of heat. It is usually expressed as a kilocalorie, which is the amount of heat needed to raise the temperature of one kilogram of water one degree Celsius. In reference to food, a calorie measures the amount of energy the food gives the consumer as it passes through the body. The body uses calories to stay alive as well as for physical activity.

Overweight and Obese

The terms *obese* and *overweight* are often used interchangeably, but health experts point out that technically there is a difference. The term *overweight* refers to increased body weight relative to height based on some standard, such as the height-weight tables found in doctors' offices. People who are overweight may or may not have excess fat. Obesity is strictly defined as an excessive amount of body fat in relation to lean body mass. This category of disease is generally further broken down into subdivisions of mild, moderate, and morbid (or severe) obesity. The classifications are not strictly defined among medical experts, but usually morbid obesity means that an individual is at least one hundred pounds over their ideal weight and is likely to develop major medical or physical problems related to the condition. The other categories may vary on the basis of body-fat distribution, age, number of pounds overweight, degree of medical risk, and degree of control an individual has over eating. Different doctors tend to focus on different aspects of these values in defining individual cases. For example, since researchers have determined that excess fat in the abdomen is medically more risky than excess fat in the hips or legs, a doctor is more likely to classify someone with a lot of excess abdominal fat as moderately or severely obese because of the risk factor.

The measurement most commonly used to differentiate between being obese and being overweight is the body mass index (BMI) This is a number that indicates body weight relative to height. The formula for BMI is the weight in pounds divided by the height in inches squared, times 703. For example, someone who is six foot three inches tall and weighs 220 pounds has a BMI of 27.5. BMI can also be calculated using kilograms and meters. This formula is the weight in kilograms divided by the height in meters squared, times ten thousand. BMI below 18.5 is considered underweight, between 18.5 and 24.9 is considered normal, between 25 and 29.9 is overweight, over 30 is obese, and over 40 is morbidly obese.

Other Measurements

Although BMI is most commonly employed to determine whether someone is overweight or obese, there are other indices used to calculate these conditions. Doctors often use insurance-company-generated height-weight tables to make

Determining Your
Body Mass Index (BMI)

The table below has already done the math and metric conversions. To use the table, find the appropriate height in the left-hand column. Move across the row to the given weight. The number at the top of the column is the BMI for that height and weight.

BMI (kg/m)	19	20	21	22	23	24	25	26	27	28	29	30	35	40
Height (inches)							Weight (pounds)							
58	91	96	100	105	110	115	119	124	129	134	138	143	167	191
59	94	99	104	109	114	119	124	128	133	138	143	148	173	198
60	97	102	107	112	118	123	128	133	138	143	148	153	179	204
61	100	106	111	116	122	127	132	137	143	148	153	158	185	211
62	104	109	115	120	126	131	136	142	147	153	158	164	191	218
63	107	113	118	124	130	135	141	146	152	158	163	169	197	225
64	110	116	122	128	134	140	145	151	157	163	169	174	204	232
65	114	120	126	132	138	144	150	156	162	168	174	180	210	240
66	118	124	130	136	142	148	155	161	167	173	179	186	216	247
67	121	127	134	140	146	153	159	166	172	178	185	191	223	255
68	125	131	138	144	151	158	164	171	177	184	190	197	230	262
69	128	135	142	149	155	162	169	176	182	189	196	203	236	270
70	132	139	146	153	160	167	174	181	188	195	202	207	243	278
71	136	143	150	157	165	172	179	186	193	200	208	215	250	286
72	140	147	154	162	169	177	184	191	199	206	213	221	258	294
73	144	151	159	166	174	182	189	197	204	212	219	227	265	302
74	148	155	163	171	179	186	194	202	210	218	225	233	272	311
75	152	160	168	176	184	192	200	208	216	224	232	240	279	319
76	156	164	172	180	189	197	205	213	221	230	238	246	287	328

this assessment. These tables list a range of acceptable weights for people of a particular height, body frame, and gender. This ends up allowing a fairly wide range of weights for people of the same height, depending on whether their body frame is large, medium, or small. For example, according to the tables published by one insurance company, a man six feet tall with a small frame ideally weighs between 149 and 160 pounds. A man of this height with a medium frame should weigh between 157 and 170 pounds and one with a large frame between 164 and 188 pounds. Someone who weighs more than these specified ranges is considered to be overweight or obese, depending on how much over they are.

Source: www.consumer.gov/weightloss/bmi.htm

Risk of Associated Disease According to BMI and Waist Size

BMI		Waist less than or equal to 40" for men or 35" for women	Waist greater than 40" for men or 35" for women
18.5 or less	Underweight	—	—
18.5 – 24.9	Normal	—	—
25.0 – 29.9	Overweight	Increased	High
30.0 – 34.9	Obese	High	Very High
35.0 – 39.9	Obese	Very High	Very High
40 or greater	Extremely Obese	Extremely High	Extremely High

Another measurement sometimes used to gauge obesity and its related health risks is the waist circumference measurement. This value is taken to determine whether the amount of abdominal fat is sufficient to put someone at risk of developing type 2 diabetes, high blood pressure, or cardiovascular disease. If a man has a waist circumference of forty inches or more and a woman has one that is thirty-five inches or more, and their BMI is higher than twenty-five, they are considered at increased risk.

The waist-to-hip ratio is another measurement sometimes used to gauge obesity. This is the ratio of a person's waist circumference to hip circumference. A waist-to-hip ratio of one or higher is considered risky for the development of heart disease. A waist-to-hip ratio of .90 or less is considered safe for men and .80 or less is considered safe for women.

Many physicians believe that simply measuring inches, weight, and height and plugging these values into a formula does not give a true assessment of whether someone is overweight, obese, or at risk for various medical problems, so they employ techniques that directly measure fat content of the body. These methods are known as anthropometry. Some anthropometry techniques use instruments called calipers to measure the thickness of skin folds in various places on the body. These methods operate under the assumption that the thickness of the skin folds represents the fatness of the entire body.

Other ways of measuring body-fat content include underwater weighing and bioelectric impedance analysis (BIA). Underwater weighing weighs the person in water to calculate body density. It yields a measurement of the percent of body fat relative to weight. With BIA, a small electrical current is run throughout the body and its resistance is measured at various points to assess fat content. Lean body tissue conducts electricity to a greater degree than fat does. Therefore, by measuring how much electrical current a particular body conducts, doctors can tell how much fat the person has.

There are also several new, high-tech ways of measuring body fat. These include dual-energy X-ray absorptiometry (DXA), total body electrical conductivity (TOBEC), and near-infrared interactance (NIR). DXA instruments use two intensities of X-rays to differentiate between lean soft tissue, fat soft tissue, and bone. TOBEC measures body composition through the use of an electromagnetic field. Measurements in TOBEC are done by inserting the person into a tubular device containing coiled wire. When electricity passes through the wire, it sends a mild current through the individual. The device measures how much electricity the body conducts. NIR uses an infrared light wand to determine fat content and is based on the principles of light absorption and reflection. The light wand sends a low-energy beam of near-infrared light through the biceps muscle in the upper arm. Depending on how much fat and muscle are present in the biceps, the light is reflected or absorbed in differing amounts. A detector in the wand measures how much light is emitted after it passes through the biceps. This value is then plugged into a formula to calculate the percentage of body fat. All of these methods are considered reliable indications of body-fat content.

The Bottom Line

Whichever measurements are used to calculate being overweight and obese, experts say that as of 2003 in the United States there are about 127 million overweight adults, about 60 million obese

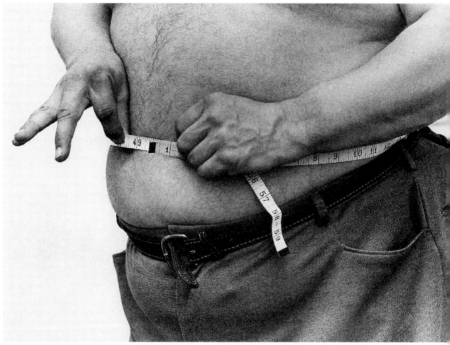

The circumference of the waist is only one measurement used to gauge obesity. Other measurements considered include body mass and body-fat content.

adults, and about 9 million morbidly obese adults. These numbers have never been higher, and they continue to grow each year. In general, women are more likely to be obese than men, and people in lower socioeconomic groups are seven times more likely to be obese than those in higher socioeconomic groups. Education level also appears to play a role, as those with less education are more likely to be obese or overweight.

Race and ethnicity also play a role in obesity. African Americans, American Indians, and Hispanic Americans have a higher rate of obesity than do Caucasian Americans, and Asian Americans have a lower prevalence of obesity. African American and Hispanic American women with low incomes seem to be at highest risk for obesity. Americans of English, Scottish, and Irish descent tend to have a lower risk of obesity than do those descended from eastern and southern European countries. Experts believe this is probably due to genetic as well as lifestyle factors.

In other places in the world, the incidence of being overweight and obese varies among particular groups. However, it is also at an all-time high, though the definition of these terms may vary among different cultures. While being overweight or obese in the United States is generally viewed as undesirable because of perceived standards of beauty that equate thinness with attractiveness, and because of concerns about the effects of obesity on health, in other cultures, this may not be the case. Medical ex-

Using calipers, a nurse measures the thickness of a patient's skin to determine his body-fat content.

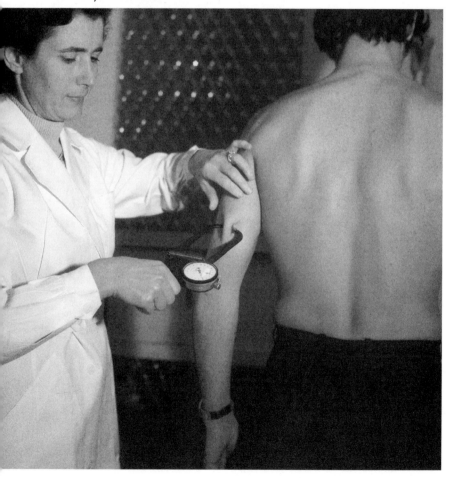

perts in certain cultures may not perceive obesity to be a condition that warrants concern. In the Efik tribe of Nigeria, for instance, fatness is seen as beautiful. Young girls in this society are housed in fattening huts for up to two years before they marry to make them as beautiful as possible. The future husband provides the best foods available for his future bride. In New Guinea, men who are leaders are admired for their large body size. In the Bemba tribe in South Africa, obese men are seen as being economically successful and possessing the spiritual powers to withstand sorcerers' attacks, so obesity is considered positive there too.

Health Problems and Obesity

Even among cultures where obesity is seen as desirable, there is increasing evidence linking it to a variety of serious health problems. In the United States, such medical problems have been well documented, and experts know that obesity causes over three hundred thousand preventable deaths each year and accounts for over $100 billion in annual medical costs. According to the Centers for Disease Control and Prevention, "Although our society has made great strides in reducing other threats to health such as smoking, we have been unable to stem the rising tide of obesity in the population. This trend is particularly disturbing because obesity is central to the development of many chronic diseases such as type 2 diabetes, heart disease, hypertension, and cancer."[4]

Type 2 Diabetes

Type 2 diabetes mellitus, a disease in which the body is not able to properly metabolize sugar, is one of the most common ailments to affect overweight and obese people. It was once considered strictly an adult disease, but now many obese children and adolescents are affected too. Health experts are especially concerned about this trend because diabetes can lead to many serious complications, such as blindness, limb amputation, and kidney disease, and the longer someone has the disease, the higher the risk of these complications.

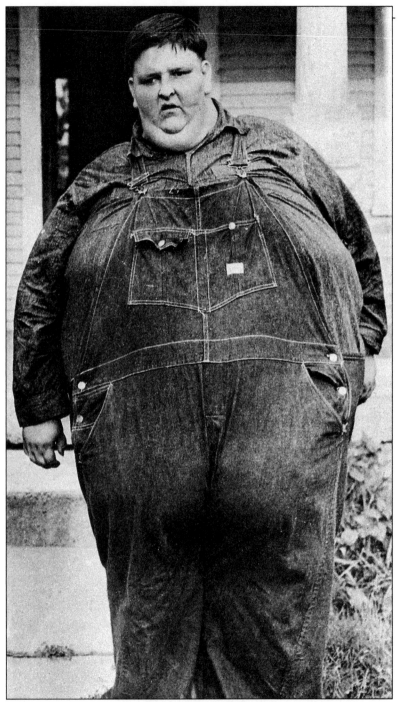

Obese people like this man are at high risk of developing a number of serious medical conditions, including heart disease and type 2 diabetes.

Type 2 diabetes is three to five times more prevalent among obese persons than in those of normal weight. The tendency to develop it increases the heavier the individual gets. Unlike in type 1 diabetes where the pancreas does not produce insulin, in type 2 diabetes, the pancreas does manufacture insulin. However, the body becomes resistant to the insulin, so the person must either inject additional synthetic insulin or take oral medication to allow the body to use whatever insulin is being produced.

Insulin is a hormone that is essential for allowing cells to take up glucose, the form of sugar that nourishes cells, from the bloodstream. Without insulin, these cells starve and glucose builds up in the blood, eventually leading to a diabetic coma and death unless treated.

Even when someone with diabetes takes medicine, fluctuations in blood-sugar levels often damage blood vessels and nerves and lead to eye, kidney, blood vessel, and nerve complications. Experts say that many obese people with type 2 diabetes would improve or even be cured of the condition if they would simply lose weight.

High Blood Pressure and Heart Disease

Being overweight or obese also commonly causes high blood pressure and heart disease. Blood pressure results from the heart pumping blood to the arteries. The pressure is the force of the blood pushing against the walls of these arteries. It is highest each time the heart beats and pumps blood and lowest when the heart is at rest between beats. Measuring this pressure is done with an instrument called a sphygmomanometer. A nurse or doctor wraps a blood-pressure cuff around the patient's upper arm and inflates the cuff with air to stop the blood flow for a few seconds. Then they open a valve on the sphygmomanometer to release air from the cuff and listen through a stethoscope to the sounds of the blood rushing through the artery.

The first sound heard and registered on the mercury column gauge of the instrument is the systolic pressure. This is the highest pressure and occurs as the blood begins to flow when the heart pumps. The second sound is the diastolic pressure, the lowest pressure, which occurs when the heart rests between beats. Blood-pressure readings are expressed as two numbers—the systolic over the diastolic pressure—and is measured in millimeters of mercury. A reading of 120/80 or less is considered good. Any reading above 140/90 is classified as high.

When blood pressure is high, the heart must work harder than normal, which makes it weaken and enlarge. This can lead to congestive heart failure, a condition where the heart can no longer pump the way it is supposed to. Uncontrolled high blood pressure can also cause the arteries to age faster than usual and to become hardened and scarred. Damaged arteries are not able to supply enough blood to organs throughout the body, and these organs may stop working properly. The kidneys, heart, and brain are especially vulnerable to damage from high blood pressure. Strokes resulting from impaired blood flow to the brain, heart attacks from blocked flow to the heart, and kidney failure from kidney artery damage are common complications. High blood pressure can be controlled with medication, but sometimes all that is necessary to lower it is for the individual to lose weight.

Besides the risk of heart disease from high blood pressure, obese people also run a much increased risk of heart disease due to high blood-fat levels. These blood fats consist of triglycerides and cholesterol. Both are produced by the liver and circulated in the blood. Triglycerides are fats that are normally elevated in the blood after digestion of fats in the intestine. But when the level of triglycerides stays elevated, this can contribute to heart disease. Cholesterol is a fat that is essential as a building material for cells in the body. But too much of it can clog the arteries, resulting in impaired circulation, chest pain, heart attack, stroke, and even sudden death. Experts point out that many of the effects of obesity and high blood-fat levels on cardiovascular health begin in childhood and progress to severe disease in adulthood. But even when someone becomes obese as an adult, heart disease is a major threat that is responsible for death in many such individuals.

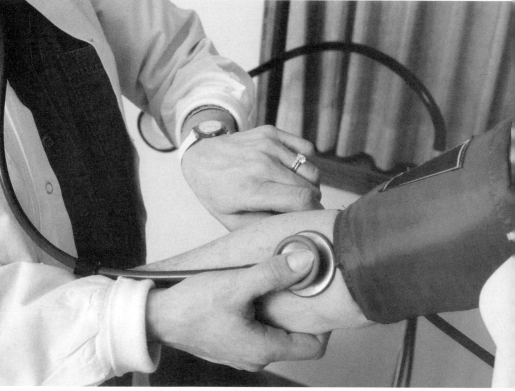

Using a stethoscope and an instrument known as a sphygmomanometer, a nurse checks a patient's blood pressure. Obesity contributes to high blood pressure.

Obesity and Cancer

In the late 1900s, medical science determined that obesity contributes to many forms of cancer. Cancer refers to a variety of conditions where unregulated cancer-cell growth kills the host organism unless successfully treated. A study published in 2003 by the *New England Journal of Medicine* in which scientists spent fifteen years evaluating nearly 1 million people concluded that excess weight contributes to more than ninety thousand cancer deaths in the United States each year. Earlier studies showed that being overweight or obese contributed to breast, uterus, colon, rectum, kidney, esophagus, and gall bladder cancers. The new study also linked being overweight or obese to cancers of the cervix, ovaries, pancreas, liver, stomach, and prostate, as well as multiple myeloma and non-Hodgkin's lymphoma.

The researchers say that having too much fat can contribute to cancer in several ways. Since excess fat increases the amount of the female hormone estrogen in the blood, it puts women at increased risk for cancers in the female reproductive system, including the breasts, ovaries, and uterus.

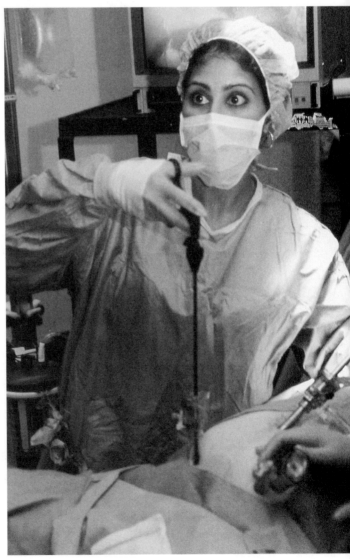

Obese people are at greater risk for many types of cancer. Here, a surgeon operates on a woman with cancer of the cervix.

Excess fat also increases the risk of acid reflux, a condition in which stomach acid spews up into the esophagus thereby increasing the risk of cancer of the esophagus. Excess fat also raises levels of insulin in the body, since more insulin is produced to process excessive amounts of food, and this in turn stimulates cell growth. This can contribute to the out-of-control growth that characterizes cancer cells. Insulin can also contribute to cancer in another way; the insulin resistance that afflicts many obese people has been linked to cancers of the colon, rectum, breast, and pancreas. Another way that obesity can trigger cancer is by impairing the immune system. This makes the person less able to defend against cancer and other invading organisms.

Doctors point out that obesity makes cancers harder to diagnose, since many forms of cancer present themselves as lumps or bumps that cannot be seen in obese people. Diagnostic tests like MRIs (magnetic resonance imaging) are difficult to perform on obese people. This is because an MRI requires placement in a narrow, cylindrical, imaging device, and many obese people simply will not fit.

Obesity makes cancers more difficult to treat, since it is harder to operate on an obese person or to fit them into radiation-therapy machines. It also makes it harder for a physician to gauge chemotherapy dosages, since fat can absorb these medications. So not only does obesity contribute to a greater risk of many types of cancer, obese people who actually get cancer have less chance of being treated successfully.

Other Health Problems

Obesity is associated with many other health problems that can be life threatening, painful, or otherwise impair normal functioning. All kinds of pain, particularly that associated with the joints, bones, muscles, and feet, are much more common among obese people. Arthritis, a variety of conditions where the body attacks its own tissue resulting in pain and disability, is very common because the entire body is under extra strain due to the excessive weight. The hips, back, knees, and feet are most often affected by this process. The wrists and hands can also be impacted; experts

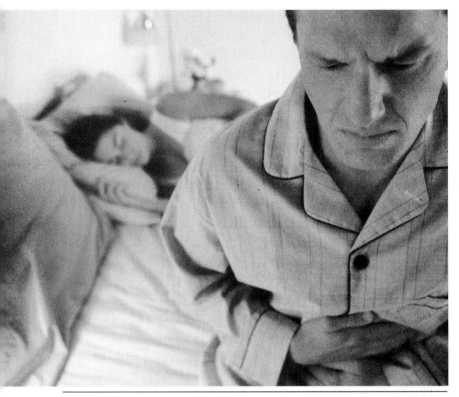

A stomach condition known as acid reflux disturbs a man's sleep. Obese people have a higher incidence of acid reflux and, as a result, a higher risk of developing cancer of the esophagus.

report that carpal tunnel syndrome, a condition where the carpal tunnel in the wrist becomes inflamed, has a higher prevalence among obese people.

Other conditions that are more common in obese people include leg ulcers, blood clots, hernias, inflammation of the pancreas, infertility, menstrual disorders, increased infections due to poor circulation and a less efficient immune system, complications from pregnancy, increased birth defects in offspring, certain psychiatric disorders such as depression, daytime sleepiness and fatigue, gout (a painful condition that results from the deposit of uric acid crystals in joints), gallstones (that result from chunks of cholesterol building up in the gallbladder), and respiratory (or breathing) problems. Respiratory problems can consist simply of shortness of breath or may progress to the point that the person needs an oxygen tank to breathe at all. This is because the lungs of obese people do not work properly due to the strain placed on them. Under the burden of having so much fat in the chest muscles, the lungs cannot expand and take in oxygen in a normal manner, and this results in an abnormally low amount of oxygen in the blood. Other respiratory conditions commonly associated with obesity are asthma, where the airways constrict so as not to allow normal breathing, and Pickwickian syndrome, also known as obesity hyperventilation syndrome or obesity sleep apnea. With Pickwickian syndrome, so named for a character called Joe the Fat Boy in the Charles Dickens novel *Pickwick Papers*, the person may fall asleep at inappropriate times, retain high levels of carbon dioxide in the lungs since the lungs do not expel this substance properly, appear bluish in color, develop heart failure due to enlargement of the heart, and experience sleep apnea, where they stop breathing hundreds of times during sleep. This condition may be life threatening in many cases.

With all of these health problems known to be associated with obesity, experts have made it a priority to educate the public about the risks. Still, the incidence of obesity continues to rise, resulting in more medical problems and expenses each year despite warnings about the consequences of being obese.

Chapter 2

What Causes Obesity?

E XPERTS AND LAYPEOPLE alike once thought that simply taking in more calories than are expended caused a person to become obese. However, scientists have determined that there are many factors—including genetics, the environment, and behavior—that contribute to obesity in varying degrees for different people.

The Role of Genetics

Genes are the part of a DNA molecule that pass hereditary information from parents to their offspring. They reside on wormlike bodies called chromosomes in the center, or nucleus, of each cell. The sequence of genes on each chromosome provides the cell containing those chromosomes with a set of instructions on how to grow and operate. Humans have forty-six chromosomes in each cell. Twenty-three come from the mother and the other twenty-three from the father. The genes on each chromosome also come in pairs, with one copy of every gene from the mother and one from the father.

When a gene or chromosome is damaged, the resulting change is called a mutation. The damage that produces a mutation can involve an entire chromosome, one or more genes, or one or more of the chemicals that make up DNA. Any of this mutated genetic material can be passed to a child if it happens to be part of the sets of chromosomes and genes transmitted from either the mother or father. When this happens, the altered genetic instructions may cause various malfunctions that produce certain diseases or disorders.

Genes and Obesity

Unlike some disorders where abnormal genes directly cause a particular condition, with obesity, the situation is more complex. Genes do not make a person fat or thin. They merely determine which individuals are more or less susceptible to weight gain due to a variety of factors, but the weight gain will not occur unless certain behavioral and environmental conditions are present. Examples of behavioral factors include eating too much and

This model shows a section of a DNA molecule. The genes in DNA may make some people susceptible to obesity.

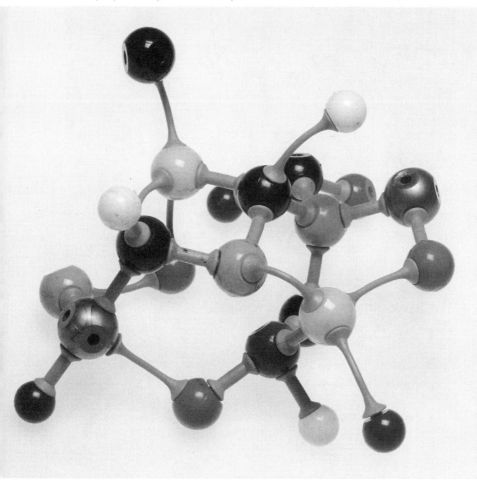

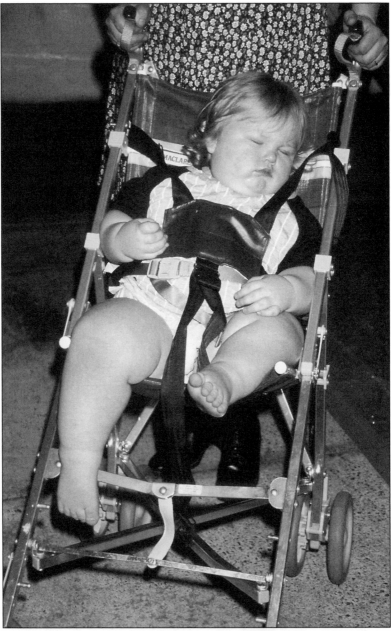

This eighteen-month-old boy weighs sixty-eight pounds. Infant obesity is often caused by a genetic mutation that creates imbalances in body chemistry.

leading an inactive lifestyle. Examples of environmental conditions are having high-fat foods available in profusion and living in a culture that encourages overindulgence.

In some cases, a genetic mutation will lead to behavior that produces obesity; for example, a disease called Prader-Willi syndrome leads a person to consume enormous quantities of food, which results in extreme obesity. First described in 1956 by Andrea Prader and Heinrich Willi, along with Alexis Labhart and Guido Fanconi, this disease affects a baby early in fetal development. The baby has feeding problems from birth on, along with short stature and a degree of mental retardation. Someone with Prader-Willi syndrome also has personality problems and is prone to temper tantrums, particularly if food is withheld. If food is not withheld, though, the individual will eat compulsively and become severely obese.

Other genetic mutations may lead to imbalances in brain chemicals and body hormones that directly influence food intake and therefore may cause obesity. Several abnormalities that can cause such imbalances are Cushing's syndrome, a disease involving overproduction of the hormone cortisol by the adrenal glands located at the base of the kidneys; hyperinsulinism, where malignant or nonmalignant tumors in the pancreas cause too much insulin to be secreted; and hypothyroidism, a condition where the thyroid gland in the neck does not produce enough thyroid hormone to properly regulate weight. The most common of these is hypothyroidism, which can be corrected by giving the affected person doses of artificial thyroid hormone to correct the imbalance. However, doctors say that even this condition is rare and is not responsible for most instances of obesity, though it is common for many obese people to try to blame an underactive thyroid gland for their fatness. Says Dr. Norman B. Ackerman in his book *Fat No More,* "Through the years I have seen only three morbidly obese patients with thyroid abnormalities."[5]

A Tendency to Store Fat

Unlike the rare cases of obesity where specific genetic abnormalities underlie the tendency to develop the condition, the majority of cases results from a genetic predisposition to gain weight and store fat. Again, in order for the weight and fat gain to occur, the person must consume too many calories, but the genetic tendency toward obesity may explain why some people are able to easily maintain or lose weight while others are not.

Experts believe that the capacity to store fat evolved in some humans over thousands of years. Until relatively recently, when food became abundant, those whose bodies were efficient at storing fat in times of famine had an advantage over those who did not. They were less likely to succumb to starvation or malnutrition, and having some extra body fat also made it more likely that a woman could bear children, another survival advantage from an evolutionary standpoint.

Indeed, many experts who have argued that obesity is not a result of an individual's weakness for overconsumption of food have pointed to the argument that genetic selection is in fact the responsible variable. According to the Centers for Disease Control and Prevention:

> People who are affected with overweight and obesity are often victims of stigmatization and discrimination. It is time to stop blaming the victim. Many obesity researchers believe that people who struggle with their weight are pushing against thousands of years of evolution that has selected [genes] for storing energy as fat in times of plenty for use in times of scarcity.[6]

The fact that many obese people have family members who are also obese supports the notion that certain genes that have been handed down within a family are at least partially responsible for the condition. While some experts have argued that this may be due to behavioral factors, such as family members sharing a high-fat diet, research on identical twins lends support to the role of genes in producing a tendency toward obesity. Identical twins have identical genes, and studies show that identical twins who do not live together have more similar eating habits and weights than do fraternal twins, who do not share identical genes.

Which Genes Play a Role in Obesity?

Since the mid-1990s, scientists have made progress in identifying some of the genes that contribute to obesity. These genes influence the tendency to gain weight and store fat in a variety of ways. Some influence the amount of certain hormones that regulate food intake and how food is processed in the body. One of the best-known genes of this type is called the ob gene. Ob encodes a hormone known as leptin. Leptin normally serves as a signal from fat cells to the brain, telling the brain that the body has eaten enough. Leptin was discovered by a team of researchers led by Dr. Jeffrey Friedman at Rockefeller University in New York in 1994. Friedman and his colleagues found that the brain believes the body is still hungry in laboratory animals

Studies of cases of obesity in identical twins, like the twins pictured here, show that genetic makeup can indeed determine a tendency toward obesity.

where the ob gene is defective and the animals do not produce leptin. This leads the animals to overeat and become obese.

When the researchers gave the leptin-deficient animals leptin artificially, the animals lost weight. Doctors initially thought that a solution for obese people was just around the corner, but it was not that simple. Scientists found that most obese people are not leptin deficient, so it appears that, at least in humans, other genes and hormones as well play an important role in obesity.

One of the other genes discovered by scientists in the late twentieth century is MC4R, which stands for melanocortin 4 receptor gene. MC4R governs a type of receptor in the area of the brain known as the hypothalamus. This area plays a role in controlling appetite. Studies have shown that over 5 percent of severely obese people have mutations in the MC4R gene. These mutations lead to too few MC4R receptors, which in turn leads to overeating. Those who inherit a copy of the defective gene from both parents showed higher degrees of obesity than did those with only one copy of the gene.

Researchers found that all the people they tested who had an MC4R mutation exhibited binge-eating behavior, a condition in which the person sporadically and uncontrollably consumes huge amounts of food. Although knowing that this binge eating is probably caused by a genetic defect rather than by a weakness of character is comforting to many of the affected persons, this knowledge still does not fix the problem. Experts say that someday doctors may be able to target therapy at fixing the defective gene, thereby alleviating the cause. More research is being carried out on this gene to determine its role in obesity and methods of fixing it.

Other Modes of Gene Action

Other genes influence obesity in a variety of ways. One such mode of action is by encouraging or discouraging the formation of fat cells. Researchers at two research centers, for example, discovered two genes that prevent immature cells from developing into fat cells. Investigators at the University of Texas Southwestern Medical Center in Dallas found that a gene called insig-1 blocks the formation of new fat cells. They hypothesize that the gene is less active in some people and in some areas of the body, thus explaining why some individuals tend to gain fat in certain areas. At Rockefeller University in New York, another team of scientists found that a gene called foxa-2 acts in a similar manner. The researchers say that someday these genes may be artificially introduced to prevent fat-cell formation as a method of combating obesity.

Other genes regulate how much fuel the muscles use to perform various tasks. People whose muscles tend to use more fuel do not gain weight as easily as do those whose muscles use less fuel to accomplish the same task. By the same token, other genes influence how many calories the body burns just to stay alive. Depending on the particular individual, breathing and other essential functions use up a widely varying range of calories. One researcher found that this level of calorie expenditure can vary from about one thousand to three thousand calories per day.

Still other genes determine the effects of exercise on a given individual. The same amount of exercise can affect oxygen usage, muscle size, and a host of other factors that in turn affect calorie burning. So individuals whose genes give them a tendency not to expend as much energy on a given amount of exercise will be more likely to retain excess weight.

Besides these genetic influences, scientists have found that some genes determine whether or not an obese person develops complications from obesity. Some extremely overweight individuals have normal blood pressure, blood sugar, and heart function. Experts believe such people possess a set of genes that protects them from these common complications.

Environmental and Behavioral Influences

Genes that predispose people to obesity or its complications, as stated before, do not on their own make someone fat or have complications. In order to become obese, an individual must take in more calories than his or her body expends, and this behavior in turn is caused by a variety of factors.

The availability and abundance of food encourage many people to routinely overeat. This, combined with a sedentary lifestyle, results in obesity for many.

Medical experts say that one of the primary reasons for the dramatic increase in the number of obese people since the mid-1900s is that the environment is much more conducive to causing weight gain in susceptible individuals. Many of the environmental changes began with the advent of modern tools, vehicles, and other technology that has increased convenience foods—such as prepackaged meals, chips, and sweets—and decreased physical activity. "Modernization, the growth of industry and technology was introduced over 50 years ago in the Western world. Modernization has led to an abundance of food (particularly high calorie intake) and a decrease in overall physical activity, contributing to increased rates of obesity,"[7] notes the American Obesity Association.

People now lead much more sedentary lives than in past eras of history. Many people drive their cars everywhere, sit and watch television for hours each day, and sit in front of computers or video games. Modern labor-saving devices, such as dishwashers, clothes dryers and washers, and microwaves, have led to a decrease in physical energy expended in the home. Many schools in the United States do not require adequate amounts of physical education, according to obesity experts. And in the workplace, many people now have jobs that involve sitting at a desk all day.

Modern convenience and prepackaged foods also have contributed to the obesity epidemic. Experts say that the vast number of women working full-time outside the home is one force behind the increased use of high-calorie convenience foods and the subsequent rise in obesity. Many families use large quantities of these high-fat, high-sugar items, and in addition, many people eat frequently at fast-food restaurants that specialize in high-calorie foods. Several obese people have directly blamed certain fast-food chains like McDonald's for their condition, stating in lawsuits that the chain is responsible for the person's obesity. As of October 2003, whether these lawsuits will actually yield settlements or be thrown out of court remains to be seen. The fast-food chains maintain that they do not force anyone to eat their food and are therefore not responsible for the choices that obese or nonobese people make.

Another reason for the increase in obesity is that portion sizes have increased. This applies to restaurants, fast-food places, and at home. The "supersize" meals at fast-food places are particularly large, say medical experts. For example, a supersized order of french fries at McDonald's contains 160 calories and seven grams of fat more than the medium-sized order. Prior to the

Many fast foods, like these fish and chips, are high in fat and have little nutritional value. The large portions of fast-food meals make them especially fattening.

1990s, most places did not even offer these supersized options. For at-home consumption, packaged foods like chips and candy bars have also gotten bigger. Doctors suggest carefully reading nutritional information on product packages to see how much fat and calories they contain.

Not only has the preponderance of convenience foods and large portions contributed to the epidemic of obesity, but researchers are finding that the combination of foods eaten is also a contributing factor. For example, studies conducted in the late twentieth century show that laboratory rats fed fat and sugar together gain more body fat than those fed these foods separately. Scientists believe the same thing happens in humans.

Experiments also show that people who eat a high-fat diet gain weight faster than those who eat a high-carbohydrate diet with the same number of calories. And the size and frequency of food intake can also affect weight and fat gain: laboratory animals and people who consume their daily calories in two or three large meals gain more weight than those who nibble throughout the day on the same foods and numbers of calories.

Social and Personal Causes of Obesity

Social and personal variables are other types of environmental forces that can contribute to obesity. Overeating is encouraged in some cultures; for example, the stereotype of the Jewish grandmother or the Greek matriarch from the old country saying, "Eat! Eat!" is not an exaggeration in many instances, and such pressures often result in overeating and subsequent obesity in members of such ethnic groups. Mark, a man whose grandmother tried to force food on everyone who entered her house, says, "That was her way of showing you that she cared, and she was highly insulted if you didn't eat and eat and eat. I had to be rude and tell her that I was not hungry."[8]

Studies have shown in other cases that some ethnic groups have a genetic predisposition for obesity, and this predisposition, coupled with lifestyle factors, often causes people in these groups to gain weight and fat. People of eastern and southern European ancestry, for instance, have a greater tendency to gain weight than do those of northern European descent. If such individuals eat a high-calorie diet and do little or no exercise, they are likely to gain large amounts of weight.

Other research indicates that some ethnic groups with a genetic predisposition for obesity do not experience widespread obesity or complications from the condition until they begin to live a modern Western lifestyle with high-calorie foods and a sedentary existence. For example, studies have shown that aborigines in Australia who once followed a traditional hunter-gatherer lifestyle with a diet low in fat and high in fiber had little problem with obesity. But once many of these tribespeople switched to a more Western, sedentary lifestyle and diet, their incidence of obesity, high blood pressure, and type 2 diabetes skyrocketed. A similar situation exists with the American Pima Indians. Those Pima living in Mexico with a traditional, high-activity lifestyle and consuming a low-fat diet have little obesity, while Pima living in Arizona who follow a sedentary lifestyle and consume a high-fat diet have a high prevalence of obesity and type 2 diabetes.

Personal and social factors, as well as cultural influences, can contribute to obesity in some people. Eating habits followed during infancy and childhood can trigger lifelong obesity. Excessive eating during these periods results in an increase in the number of fat cells in the body. People with many fat cells have been shown to have difficulty losing weight.

Another common influence on obesity is the presence of personal and social problems. Some people tend to eat more when they are unhappy or feel rejected, and this often turns into a vicious cycle. The overweight individual feels rejected socially because of obesity, which in turn leads to more overeating, which causes the person to become even heavier. Says one obese woman who knows her weight problem has a lot to do with eating for comfort, "Whenever I feel neglected, or get angry, or sad, or . . . I eat something to feel better."[9]

Studies on whether or not obese individuals get that way in the first place due to severe emotional illness give mixed results, however. One study by psychiatrist Katherine Halmi found no evidence of a higher incidence of psychiatric illness in obese persons. But other studies have indicated a higher-than-normal incidence of such disorders, especially depression, as causative factors for the obesity. Sometimes the drugs prescribed for psychiatric disorders can contribute to obesity; examples are lithium, some antidepressants, and antipsychotic drugs.

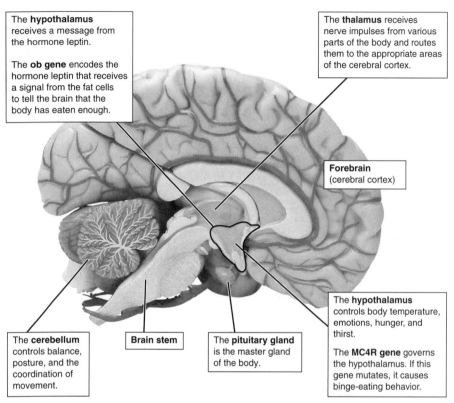

The **hypothalamus** receives a message from the hormone leptin.

The **ob gene** encodes the hormone leptin that receives a signal from the fat cells to tell the brain that the body has eaten enough.

The **thalamus** receives nerve impulses from various parts of the body and routes them to the appropriate areas of the cerebral cortex.

Forebrain (cerebral cortex)

The **hypothalamus** controls body temperature, emotions, hunger, and thirst.

The **MC4R gene** governs the hypothalamus. If this gene mutates, it causes binge-eating behavior.

The **cerebellum** controls balance, posture, and the coordination of movement.

Brain stem

The **pituitary gland** is the master gland of the body.

Doctors have identified two specific psychological disorders that cause obesity in some cases. In binge-eating disorder, an individual sporadically loses control and ingests huge quantities of food in a short time. Such people feel extremely distressed after the binge. Unlike bulimics, though, who binge eat and then force themselves to vomit, people with binge-eating disorder do not make themselves throw up and therefore gain weight from their behavior. Experts say that 10–20 percent of individuals who enter weight-reduction programs can attribute their obesity to binge-eating disorder.

Night-eating syndrome is the second psychological disorder that can cause obesity. People with this disorder rarely eat in the morning, but consume large quantities of food at night. Most have trouble sleeping, in large part because of the quantities of food they consume. Experts say that about 10 percent of people seeking to lose weight suffer from night-eating syndrome.

Factors That Contribute to Obesity

FACTORS	DESCRIPTION	RESULT
Fast-food restaurants	Super-sized portions	Increased portions add more fat and calories to a meal already high in calories and fat.
Prepackaged foods	Frozen and prepackaged foods higher in calories than fresh foods	These foods are high in fat and sugar, which increase weight.
Environmental changes	Advent of modern tools, vehicles, and other technology	Decreased physical activity and need for fewer calories increase weight.
Two to three large meals per day	Increased weight gain with large meals	There is less weight gain when eating the same calorie count with smaller meals throughout the day.
High-fat calories	High-fat calories found in red-meat products	High-fat calories increase weight significantly more than carbohydrate calories.
High carbohydrates	Carbohydrates include such foods as fresh vegetables, fruits, rice, pasta, potatoes	Eating a high-carbohydrate diet with the same calorie intake as fat-diet calories can prevent increased weight gain.
Food combinations	Fat and sugar eaten together cause weight gain	Eating fat and sugar separately can prevent weight gain.
Mutated MC4R gene	Governs the hypothalamus, one possible cause of obesity	Causes binge-eating behavior.
Mutated ob gene	Encodes the hormone leptin, one possible cause of obesity	Causes overeating when the fat cells fail to send a signal to the leptin, which notifies the hypothalamus that the body has eaten enough .
Insig-1 gene	University of Texas Southwestern Medical Center hypothesizes that the gene is less active in some people and in some areas of the body	This gene blocks the formation of new fat cells.
Foxa-2 gene	Rockefeller University in New York found this gene to act as insig-1 gene	This gene blocks the formation of new fat cells.
Other genes	Influence how many calories the body burns to exist	The level of calorie expenditure can vary from about one thousand to three thousand calories.

A Variety of Causes

Whether social factors, genes, or certain behaviors are involved in causing obesity, it is apparent that the answer to the question of what causes it is not a simple one. For most obese people, no single factor is responsible for their condition. Most likely it is a combination of a genetic predisposition and a variety of behavioral, social, personal, or cultural influences that lead to the excess fat and weight gain that characterize obesity.

Chapter 3

How Is Obesity Treated?

PEOPLE USE MANY methods to try to treat obesity by losing weight. Different techniques work best for different individuals, and in some cases an obese person must try a variety of strategies before finding one that helps. Sometimes nothing seems to work, and the person remains unable to either lose weight or keep it off, no matter what they try.

The National Heart, Lung, and Blood Institute stresses that any viable weight-loss program should focus on long-term goals. "Remember, quick weight loss methods don't provide lasting results. Weight loss methods that rely on diet aids like drinks, prepackaged foods, or diet pills don't work in the long run. Whether you lose weight on your own or with a group, remember that the most important changes are long-term."[10] These long-term changes include making lifestyle adjustments that incorporate healthy eating and exercise into everyday life so that a healthy weight can be maintained over the long run.

Goals of Treatment

Whichever method of weight loss is used, the goals of treatment are similar. It once was that physicians and other experts who designed treatment programs tried to help an obese person achieve their ideal weight based on official height-weight charts. But most obese people could not achieve this goal, so experts gradually modified the goals of treatment. Today, most programs aim for what is known as the 10 percent solution—to lose about 10 percent of body weight as a method of reducing the complications of obesity. This focuses on managing weight in the context of overall health rather than setting a goal of attaining what is considered an ideal weight, though many obese individuals do end up choosing to lose more than the recommended 10 percent as a method of looking and feeling their best.

Doctors say that the best way to lose any amount of weight is slowly, at a rate of one to two pounds per week, to be safe. A gradual weight loss also helps keep the weight off permanently. Reducing caloric intake by five hundred calories per day generally results in a one pound per week weight loss.

Experts recommend keeping track of calories consumed and expended to help reliably achieve a gradual weight loss. This

Most successful weight-loss programs encourage lifestyle adjustments, such as healthier eating and exercise, that result in gradual and permanent weight loss.

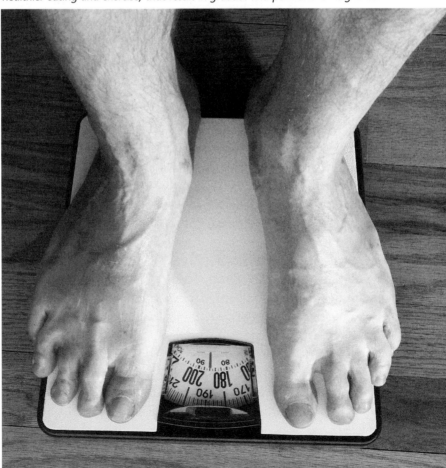

involves tabulating foods eaten and portion sizes in addition to calories expended in daily exercise and activities. The number of calories expended should exceed the number taken in so weight loss can occur. Charts listing the number of calories in certain foods are readily available from a variety of sources. In order to calculate the number of calories expended, the number of calories used in various activities must be added to the basal metabolic rate (BMR), a measurement of the number of calories needed to live while resting. BMR depends on age, body type, degree of obesity, the amount of thyroid hormone produced, body temperature, environmental temperature, and a host of other factors. There are several formulas available for calculating BMR based on height, weight, and age. To find out how much energy is expended during certain activities, doctors and exercise authorities have charts that detail these values. The number of calories expended during a particular activity varies slightly from person to person depending on body composition and effort put forth, so these values are not accurate to the letter, but they do offer a good idea of energy expenditure.

Methods of Losing Weight

Whether the emphasis is on counting calories, increasing exercise, or other factors, there are four basic types of treatment available for obesity: diet and nutritional counseling, behavior therapy, drugs, and surgery.

The most common, and the first line of treatment, is dieting. Although special diets for weight reduction were unusual until the nineteenth and twentieth centuries, they did exist before that time. One early example is the Greek physician Hippocrates recommending a diet high in fatty foods to feel full and so the body would grow tired of fat. Hippocrates also recommended that an obese person eat only once a day to help lose weight. Doctors now know that fatty foods do not necessarily make a person feel full, nor do they make the individual grow tired or fat. Eating once a day is also known to be unhealthy.

Another early diet plan was conceived in 1558 by the obese Luigi Cornaro of Italy, who put himself on a diet that included twelve ounces of food and fourteen ounces of liquid per day. Cornaro lost weight on this plan, his health improved, and he lived to be ninety-one years old. His book *A Treatise of the Benefits of a Sober Life* was one of the first diet books ever published.

The Scottish physician George Cheyne was another notable early diet book author. He wrote several books in the early 1700s about his experiences with different diets. Cheyne, who had shortness of breath, asthma, and stomach problems, tried various diets and medications to lose weight. He tried a milk diet and lost weight, but eventually gained it back. Finally, he followed a vegetarian diet that he consumed with milk, tea, and coffee and was able to keep the weight off and improve his health.

In the 1860s, William Banting of London popularized a diet consisting mostly of lean meat, dry toast, soft-boiled eggs, and green vegetables. He lost over fifty pounds, and his book *Letter on Corpulence* describing his diet became famous in England and America. His method of dieting became known as the "banting."

Modern Diets

After the early weight-loss diets, an entire dieting industry developed during the twentieth century, with every imaginable variety of solutions offered. Some diets stress high protein, others high carbohydrate or low fat. Some even suggest an all-liquid diet, and others offer a combination of approaches. While the best approach varies by individual, doctors say that any diet should provide adequate nutrition while involving intake of less food than the person's energy requirements. Ideally, an effective diet should be one that can be sustained long term to prevent medical problems and the yo-yo effect of weight loss and gain that so many dieters experience. That is why most experts caution against "fad" diets, which overemphasize one food or type of food, since they do not provide balanced nutrition. Such fad diets include the grapefruit diet, the cabbage soup diet, the no-carbohydrate diet, and so on.

The near-starvation or "crash" diets that some people attempt are also not recommended by most medical authorities. People who follow these types of diets may lose some weight but will

The ancient Greek physician Hippocrates (seated, left) prescribed one of the earliest known diets. He advised his patients to eat fatty foods to make them feel full and cause them to eat less.

probably gain it right back when they begin eating again. They also can experience serious health risks and even death if the diet is extreme. These crash or starvation diets limit calories severely to four hundred to eight hundred calories per day. They include liquid protein diets and various semifasting regimens like Optifast and Medifast. Doctors say these plans are so risky that they may require hospitalization so the diet can be conducted under direct medical supervision, if the person elects to follow the plan. The Food and Drug Administration warns, "Very low calorie diets are not without risk and should be pursued only under medical supervision. Unsupervised, very low calorie diets can deprive you of important nutrients and are potentially dangerous."[11]

The lack of nutritional balance in these extreme diets can lead to chemical imbalances of elements like potassium, magnesium, and phosphorus, even if vitamin and mineral supplements are taken. Dizziness, fatigue, headache, muscle cramps, rashes, dry skin, bad breath, and gastrointestinal upsets are common side effects. Heart irregularities are responsible for many of the deaths attributed to these very-low-calorie diets.

Most experts recommend what are known as conventional, well-balanced diets for safe weight loss. These diets limit calories to between twelve hundred and two thousand calories per day.

In addition to exercising, most weight-loss experts recommend limiting caloric intake, eating a wide variety of foods, and drinking plenty of water.

Some emphasize certain types of foods or combinations, and most require drinking lots of water.

Self-Help Groups

Many people who are dieting choose to attend one or more of any of a number of self-help groups that have been set up to prescribe diets and give support to people trying to lose weight. Examples are Weight Watchers, Take Off Pounds Sensibly (TOPS), and Overeaters Anonymous. Overeaters Anonymous is based on the principles of Alcoholics Anonymous. Such groups seek to provide support to those who have an addiction like alcohol, or, in the case of obesity, food. Other self-help groups tend to provide group sessions, counselors, meal plans, dietary education, and even specially packaged foods. Many people find they benefit from the social setting and shared experiences provided by such groups. People lose varying amounts of weight; some keep it off, especially if they continue to attend meetings that follow the program, while others quit and may gain back whatever weight they lose.

The National Heart, Lung, and Blood Institute recommends some guidelines for choosing one of these weight-loss programs. Questions to ask include finding out about the quality of the counselors, supervision by physicians or registered dieticians, availability of long-term counseling or a support system after the program ends, quality of the food choices, and whether or not the goals and rules are realistic. Prospective clients should also find out how many people successfully complete the program, their average weight loss, and fees for services and items like dietary supplements.

Why Diets May Not Work

Whether an obese person tries to lose weight using a self-help group diet plan, through a medically supervised diet, or simply on their own, the fact is that many times diets do not work for several reasons. One reason is that many people do not stick with the diet for long enough to make a difference. Another is that, in some people, the body is very efficient at trying to maintain a particular weight and level of fat. This level is called the set point. Some peoples' bodies work hard to maintain this set point. For example, in one experiment, a group of people who were consuming fewer calories than usual showed a 15 percent drop in energy expenditure. This meant that their bodies were burning fewer calories in response to taking in fewer calories. This made it nearly impossible for these individuals to lose weight by cutting calories and dieting alone.

Researchers, though, have found that it is possible to reset the set point. This can be achieved by changing the type of foods consumed—from rich, fatty foods to low-fat, low-sugar choices—and by increasing the level of physical activity. This is why most diet programs also include an exercise program. The best type of exercise for helping to lose weight requires the whole body to move, as in walking, jogging, or swimming. Experts emphasize the importance of incorporating such exercise into a daily routine, as well as making small lifestyle adjustments like climbing stairs instead of taking an elevator and parking farther away from a destination to get in more walking.

Behavior Modification Programs

Making changes like incorporating exercise and following a reduced-calorie diet are examples of behavior modification techniques designed to help obese people lose weight. Such changes can be part of a formal behavior modification program, which is the second major type of weight loss strategy, or may just be undertaken by an individual as part of an informal program in their quest to lose weight.

Formal behavior modification programs treat obesity as a learned disorder. Such programs seek to change an individual's behavior so they behave like a nonobese person. The idea is that this will facilitate weight loss. Often these programs are administered by psychologists who specialize in the treatment of eating disorders. Sometimes self-help groups like Weight Watchers incorporate these techniques into their weight-loss plans.

Some behavior modification programs teach patients to carefully monitor the number of calories they ingest. They may also

Most weight-loss strategies include exercise programs that require the whole body to move, such as walking, jogging, or swimming.

involve teaching the person the behavior of eating very slowly or of eating only in a certain place in the house. Some programs prohibit eating in front of the television to prevent "mindless" eating. Some plans involve rewards, such as money, for people who successfully modify their behavior and lose weight, and some require a certain amount and type of exercise each day. In many cases, a therapist also counsels the individual to address issues of depression or anxiety that may underlie an eating disorder.

As with other weight-loss techniques, the success of behavior modification programs depends on a particular individual's motivation to succeed, on self-discipline, and on other factors, such as family support. Some obese people do very well in teaching themselves to change their behavior and lose weight, while others find that they are unable to make the necessary changes to succeed.

Diet Pills

The third main type of treatment for obesity involves weight-reduction drugs, or diet pills. These drugs include a variety of types, such as purgatives to empty the intestines, diuretics to promote water loss, emetics to promote vomiting, stimulants to

To succeed at losing weight, dieters must change such detrimental eating behaviors as habitual snacking in front of the television.

suppress the appetite, and others. Most of these drugs have serious side effects and must be used carefully. Amphetamines, for example, the major kind of stimulant used to suppress the appetite, often cause sleeplessness, increased heart rate and blood pressure, dizziness, tremors, headache, impotence, and hallucinations. These drugs also lose their effectiveness over time, so larger and larger doses may be required to keep promoting weight loss. They can also be psychologically and physically addictive. In some states, it is illegal for physicians to prescribe amphetamines for weight loss.

A newer group of drugs that are similar to amphetamines include Adipex, Bontril, Fastin, Prelu-2, and Tenuate. They are somewhat safer and have fewer side effects, but can still be dangerous. Most manufacturers recommend only short-term use of these drugs. Another newer drug is the well-known fenfluramine-phentermine combination (fen-phen), banned from the market in 1997 after many patients developed heart-valve damage and high blood pressure. Some patients even died while taking the drug. Fenfluramine itself was also banned, but the appetite suppressant phentermine is still on the market, since it does not appear to be dangerous when used by itself.

One of the newest prescription weight-loss drugs is sibutramine, marketed as Meridia. It works by making the user feel full and also increases the metabolism. It has adverse side effects, including raising blood pressure and heart rate, so it cannot be used by people with high blood pressure or heart problems. Another popular new drug is orlistate, marketed as Xenical. It works by blocking about 30 percent of dietary fat from being absorbed by the intestines. Sometimes this causes gastrointestinal upsets because this fat is passing through the body undigested.

Besides the prescription options, there are many weight-loss dietary supplements sold in drugstores and health-food stores and available without a prescription. These substances are not regulated by the Food and Drug Administration in the same manner as are drugs, so many people consume them thinking they are harmless. But experts point out that some of these supplements are far from harmless. For example, the American

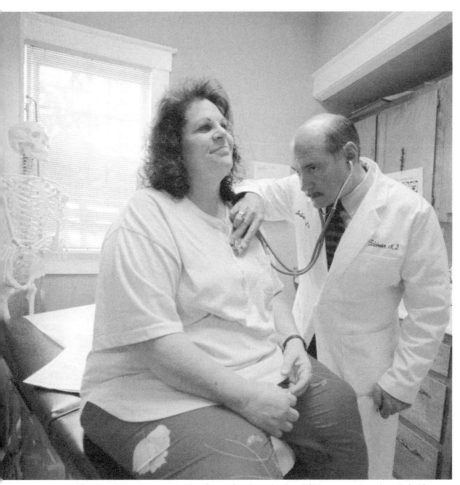

Severely obese persons who have had no luck with conventional weight-loss programs often consult with a physician about alternatives such as diet pills and bariatric surgery.

Heart Association has urged the federal government to ban the sale of ephedra, an herbal supplement often used as a weight-loss aid. Ephedra produces high blood pressure, irregular heartbeat, stroke, heart attack, and even death in some cases. After the February 2003 death of Baltimore Orioles pitcher Steve Bechler from ephedra, the Food and Drug Administration proposed the first manufacturing standards for dietary supplements, but they had not banned the substance as of October 2003.

Treatment with Surgery

For many obese people, weight-loss drugs, behavior therapy, and diets are ineffective in helping them lose weight. When this happens and there are serious health complications from the obesity, the only other option may be surgery. Surgery to treat morbid obesity is known as bariatric surgery. Doctors who perform such operations emphasize that they are not cosmetic procedures, but instead may be medically necessary to control the many health problems that often go along with severe obesity.

As Norman Ackerman, a bariatric surgeon, explains in his book *Fat No More*, surgeons used to be involved with treating only the effects of obesity rather than the obesity itself.

> Surgeons have been involved with the care of very obese patients for many years. At first, our task was to treat some of the complications of obesity. Neurosurgeons and orthopedic surgeons have treated the various back problems that plague the very obese, and orthopedists have repaired, and more recently, replaced diseased joints in the legs of these unfortunate patients. Cardiac surgeons have been operating on the hearts of obese and other patients for about forty years.[12]

Early Surgeries

In the 1950s, surgeons began to experiment with operations to treat obesity itself rather than just its effects. In 1954, Arnold Kremen and John Linner at the University of Minnesota in Minneapolis published an account of their studies on removing part of the small intestine in an obese woman to help her lose weight. The operation, known as a jejunoileal bypass or intestinal bypass, removed a section of the jejunum (the upper small intestine) and the ileum (the lower small intestine). The surgeons removed about 75 percent of the small intestine and the woman lost over thirty pounds. Later they removed more and she lost an additional seventy pounds.

Other surgeons began performing similar operations to help morbidly obese people lose weight. Some bypassed the entire ileum and connected the jejunum directly to the colon (the large intestine). Others bypassed part of the small intestine and some of the large intestine. But there were severe complications when the colon was bypassed, including nutritional deficiencies, diarrhea, and liver failure, so the so-called jejunocolic bypass was not performed for very long. The jejunoileal bypass became the most popular operation for weight loss in the 1960s and 1970s. Different surgeons believed different lengths of the jejunum and ileum should be removed to achieve the best results. The operation worked because it allowed only a fraction of the calories consumed to be absorbed by the body. Patients often experienced complications like diarrhea, poor absorption of some nutrients, liver damage, kidney stones, and nausea and vomiting, but the surgery did help many severely obese people lose weight. When the gastric bypass was invented, however, the intestinal bypass became obsolete.

The Gastric Bypass

The gastric bypass operation, also known as stomach stapling, has become the most common surgical procedure for treating obesity. It is done using stainless steel staples, stitches, or plastic or metal bands to make the part of the stomach that receives food very small so the patient will eat less. It also makes the outlet from the stomach small so that food leaves the stomach slowly and the person feels full for longer. The food goes directly from the upper part of the stomach to the intestine through an opening. The lower part of the stomach is bypassed; this is where the name gastric bypass comes from.

There are some variations on the gastric bypass. Sometimes the upper part of the stomach is made to empty into the lower stomach, so this area is not bypassed; the procedure is called a gastroplasty. Results are similar to those of the gastric bypass.

After a gastric bypass or similar operation, the patient cannot eat or drink for four or five days. Then they are allowed a liquid diet, progressing after several weeks to a normal diet. But because of the reduced size of the stomach, they can only tolerate a very small amount of food at a time. Because of this, the person loses substantial amounts of weight. One obese woman who had

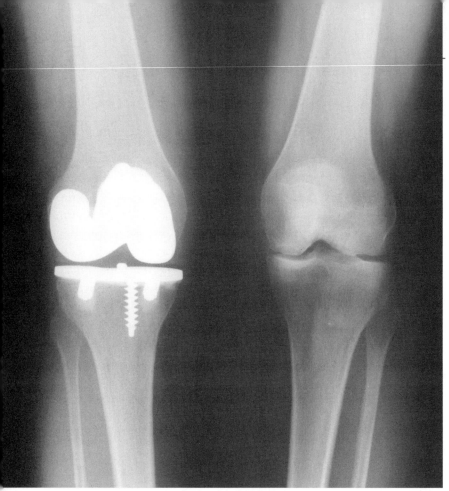

This X-ray shows a surgically replaced knee joint. Joint damage is one of many negative health effects of prolonged, extreme obesity.

a gastric bypass went from 250 pounds to 122 pounds in one year; an obese man went from 497 pounds to 232 pounds. Sometimes the weight loss is so great that plastic surgery is required to tighten up the resulting loose skin.

Even though this operation leads to substantial weight loss in many people, there are still risks and complications. One problem sometimes seen is injury to the spleen, which lies next to the stomach. Other complications may include excess bleeding, pneumonia or blood clots in the lungs after surgery, infection, vomiting, ulcers, gallstones, vitamin deficiencies, and anemia. But for the severely obese people who undergo the operation, most say the risks are worth it because it is their last resort for losing weight after other methods have failed.

Other Surgery

There is one other surgical technique often used to treat severe obesity. With jaw wiring, an oral surgeon wires the jaw shut so the patient can take in only a liquid diet through a straw. The diet usually consists of milk, fruit juice, vitamins, and sometimes liquefied soft foods.

Although patients may lose weight, the procedure has its drawbacks. Some patients complain of dry lips, sore gums, and bad breath. Also, if the patient has to vomit, they risk choking because the mouth will not open. For this reason, many doctors give these patients a set of wire cutters to use in such an emergency.

Generally the jaws remain wired shut for about six months. While most people lose significant amounts of weight, once the wires are removed, many people resume their old eating habits and begin to regain the weight they lost.

Alternative Treatment Methods

Besides the four major types of treatment for obesity, there are several alternative methods. One is spa and water cures, which have been used since as far back as the Roman Empire. These include various types of hot and cold baths and saunas. The hot baths and saunas are supposed to exert their therapeutic effects by making the person sweat off some weight, and other forms of water treatments are supposed to be healthy in general but not specifically beneficial for weight loss. While experts say that these treatments that cause sweating may result in the loss of a few pounds, most agree that water treatments are not effective for permanent or major weight loss.

Hypnotism is another alternative treatment. Here, a professional therapist hypnotizes the obese person and leaves them with the suggestion that they will be able to reduce the amount they eat when they wake up. Most people who try this method report that it is not successful in treating obesity, though there are many professional hypnotists who claim that it works.

Acupuncture, an ancient Chinese system of medicine that uses fine needles inserted at various critical points on the skin, has also been used to help with weight-reduction efforts. An acupuncturist places needles in appropriate locations to relieve hunger and suppress the appetite. Sometimes a staplelike device is placed on certain points in the outer ear and left there to accomplish the same purpose. Many patients say the technique works well, though there is little scientific data on whether acupuncture treatments effectively reduce obesity. One recent

Keeping a food diary can help manage and maintain a diet and a healthy weight.

scientific study did show that patients who received acupuncture treatments to the ear had significantly more appetite reduction and weight loss than did control subjects on the same diet and exercise plan. This led the researchers to conclude that "ear acupuncture at designated points, in conjunction with a reduced calorie diet and increased physical activity, is effective in treating obesity."[13]

Maintaining Weight Loss

Whichever methods people use to lose weight, once the desired weight loss is achieved, doctors recommend a variety of techniques for best keeping the weight off, since regaining lost weight is a common problem for the obese. Strategies include limiting intake of fast foods, eating several small meals each day instead of two or three large ones, restricting intake of fats and sugars, maintaining a regular exercise program, and taking weight measurements regularly. Keeping a food diary can also help. Many people also find that keeping fresh, low-fat foods readily available is important. So is planning what to eat in advance rather than grabbing whatever sounds good at the moment. Drinking plenty of water throughout the day also helps keep the appetite in check.

In one study of people who managed to lose sixty or more pounds and keep it off for an average of six years, the important factors seemed to be eating a low-fat diet, weighing frequently, being physically active, and eating breakfast every day.

Chapter 4

Living with Obesity

O BESITY HAS A major impact on many aspects of an individual's life, including psychological, social, overall health, and lifestyle issues. Social and emotional effects, of course, vary in different cultures, but in the United States, where thinness is perceived as attractiveness, obese people are usually seen as unattractive. This makes them the brunt of jokes and derision concerning their condition. One study found that on television, where 90 percent of female stars are underweight, overweight characters are often objects of ridicule and are perceived as lazy and lacking in self-control. Another study that is a classic in the field of social psychology originally appeared in the *Journal of Personality and Social Psychology* in 1967 and is still cited by many experts in the field. It showed that children as young as six years describe silhouettes of obese children as lazy, stupid, dirty, ugly, liars, and cheaters. This indicates that kids learn stereotypes associated with obese people early in life.

For an obese person who is the object of such ridicule and derision, the emotional effects can be devastating. One obese woman commented, "Life is so lonely when you are obese. People mock obesity and think it isn't a real disease, but they are wrong! I have seen its effects for so long and I have felt them!"[14]

One woman who gained sixty-five pounds after having a baby was amazed at how isolated and picked on she felt just because of her weight. She said:

> Since my weight gain, my life has changed so much. I used to be "quite pretty" or so my family keeps saying, but now I am just an embarrassment to them. Most of the overt discrimina-

tion that I have felt has come from my own family members. They often refuse to invite me to public places, and have even been known to take food right out of my hands during family gatherings.[15]

This woman's mother told her that as long as she was fat, her achievements would mean nothing because no one cared about fat people. Her husband refused to take her to an office party because he was afraid his coworkers would no longer respect him if he was seen with her.

This sort of attitude shows that although many professionals and organizations for the obese now regard obesity as a disease, many people still do not see it that way. Even many doctors reportedly see obese people as lazy and lacking in self-control, and a good number of doctors prefer not to treat the obese because they do not think they will get results. Says one obese woman, "The doctors, most of them seem really uncaring toward our condition, like if we really wanted to be thin we would do something about it. That's just not the case. No one wishes to be obese."[16]

Obesity and Young People

For children and teens who are obese, the teasing and isolation from their peers can be especially difficult to endure. One seventeen-year-old girl who weighed 440 pounds dropped out of school because she could not tolerate the nasty comments from other students. She was depressed, hated her body, and wished she could lose weight, but instead sat around doing nothing but eating. She wrote:

> I missed my whole teenage-hood because of my obesity. I wish I could go to a store and buy sexy clothing and bell bottoms and tank tops and a bikini, but I can't because they don't make clothing in my size. I know I'm not the only obese person in the world but me being a teenager and watching all these other skinny teenage girls, it makes me feel like I am the only one and I feel like such a freak. I wish I could change, but it's so hard. I really need some support right now. I wish all these

Obese children are typically ostracized and left with feelings of low self-esteem. One study showed that obesity carries a physical, social, and emotional impact similar to that of cancer.

pretty skinny, inshape people could just respect me, but that will never happen because of the way I look.[17]

This experience is fairly typical for many obese kids from elementary school on up. Studies have shown that children and teens identify obese kids as individuals they do not want as friends. One study of obese adolescent girls found that 96 percent experienced ostracism, teasing, and rejection on a continuous basis, which led to low self-esteem. Self-esteem was found to be lowest in those who believed they were responsible for being overweight.

One study at the University of California, San Diego, compared obese children to those with normal body weights and to children with cancer and found that obesity had a physical, social, and emotional impact similar to cancer. "The quality of life for severely obese children and adolescents is roughly equivalent to that of pediatric cancer patients undergoing chemotherapy,"[18] said the authors of the study. The obese kids were socially isolated, missed school more often than other kids, and had many more physical afflictions than normal.

Discrimination and Obesity

Besides the ostracism and rejection that many obese people feel, a large percentage also find they are routinely discriminated against in employment and other situations. Obese people are often not hired or—if they are—are not promoted, and do not receive comparable salaries to those who are not obese. According to the American Obesity Association, this discrimination seems to affect women more than men, at least where wages are concerned. One study found that the wages of mildly obese women were 5.9 percent lower than for women of normal weight. Wages for morbidly obese women were 24.1 percent lower. Men only received lower wages at the very highest weight levels.

Explains one obese woman:

> People are extremely prejudiced towards fat people. I was passed over for employment positions because of my size. For example, I was eighteen years old and weighed in at 211 pounds. I had an interview with a large corporation in Manhattan. The personnel agent told me I was not suited for the position and that before I interview again in the city that I should lose some serious weight. She told me appearance was everything, if you look sloppy they base your working habits on your appearance. Being overweight is not businesslike.[19]

In another case, John, who weighed about four hundred pounds, was fired from his job. The reason given was poor performance, but John had always done a good job and his coworkers and customers at the store where he worked said his performance was excellent. John sued his employer and was awarded over $1 million for lost compensation and emotional distress. The jury made this award because they concluded that

John was being penalized for his weight, a condition that was mostly beyond his control.

Advocates for the obese have hailed this decision as a major step forward for the rights of overweight and obese people. Although the laws of one state, Michigan, expressly prohibit employment discrimination on the basis of weight, such discrimination is not usually considered to be strictly illegal in most of the nation. The Civil Rights Act of 1964, which prohibits discrimination in employment, does not specifically list weight or obesity as a protected characteristic. The Americans with Disabilities Act, passed in 1990, prohibits employment discrimination for people who are disabled, but also does not list obesity per se as a disability. Some complications of obesity qualify as disabilities, but obesity itself does not. As more people file discrimination lawsuits, the courts will have to more clearly define whether or not obesity qualifies as a disability in some or all cases.

Despite the high incidence of discrimination and serious medical problems associated with obesity, recent research finds that most Americans do not believe that obesity itself should be treated as a disability that requires protection by the government. Many people who support legislation giving special accommodations to other serious medical conditions do not believe the obese merit such support. J. Eric Oliver and Taeku Lee, authors of a 2002 study on obesity-related legislation, write: "Most Americans continue to understand obesity as a case of individual moral failure rather than see it as the result of the food environment or genetics."[20]

Physical Limitations

Besides emotional, social, and job-related hardships, living with obesity is difficult because of the many physical problems and limitations it imposes. Not only is it difficult for the severely obese to move around; it is virtually impossible for many to exercise at all, including walking. Because of the breathing problems, foot pain, and back pain experienced by many obese people, walking even short distances may be very painful. Betty,

Activists protesting obesity discrimination perform an aerobic routine during San Francisco's Fat Freedom Fighters' "No Diet Day." Some lawsuits targeting obesity discrimination have been successful.

for example, who weighed three hundred pounds, had special shoes made to try to alleviate the pain in her feet, but still was unable to walk more than a few steps because of the discomfort.

Doris, who had two small children, lamented the fact that her 390 pounds kept her from being able to do anything with the kids like a normal mom. Her high blood pressure, diabetes, pain in her legs, feet, and back, and rashes and infections kept her practically bedridden and prevented her from leading any kind of productive life.

Physical problems can also result in the obese person having to take many medications and make frequent doctor visits. As well as being extremely expensive, all these medications can have dangerous interactions and create further health problems. Jeff, for example, took medication for high blood pressure, high cholesterol, asthma, arthritis, and gastrointestinal reflux disease. He was constantly light-headed and exhausted from the medications as well as from his health problems.

Access to Medical Care

Along with experiencing the everyday physical problems and limitations, the obese often face difficulties in obtaining all types of medical care. Something as simple as getting certain diagnostic medical tests can be impossible. One obese man died of cancer because his doctors could not perform the proper diagnostic tests, such as MRI, because he could not fit into machine Then,

Diet guru Dick Gregory (rear) interviews a candidate for his diet program. Losing weight enables obese people to enjoy normal social activities and better health.

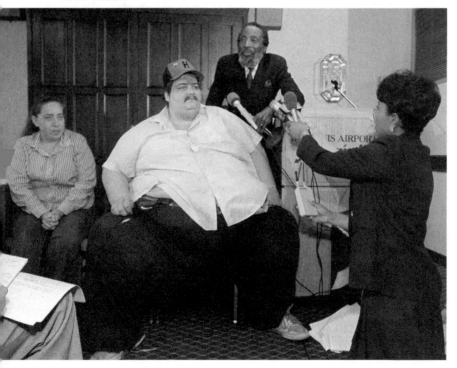

while he was in the hospital before his death, he was seriously injured when he tried to get out of bed, could not do so on his own, and fell when the nurses were unable to help him because of his bulk.

A recent study at Johns Hopkins University School of Medicine showed that obese people are less likely to seek preventive health care because of their weight. Obese women in particular tend to avoid tests like mammograms, which are used to detect breast cancer, and therefore put themselves at increased risk of not having such a condition diagnosed and treated.

When an obese person becomes ill and requires surgical treatment, the difficulties associated with excess weight are further exacerbated. For example, someone who weighs four hundred pounds will not fit on a hospital bed or gurney, so special arrangements have to be made. One woman who needed back surgery had to be weighed on a truck scale because no standard patient scale could accommodate her bulk, and her doctor needed an accurate reading so he could find an operating table that could handle her weight. Also, administering intravenous anesthesia and other medications is problematic, since it is difficult to insert an IV needle with layers of fat burying the blood vessels. Cutting through and keeping so much body fat out of the way during an operation is also a concern for surgeons.

Access to Insurance

Another problem associated with medical care concerns difficulties obese people have getting medical and life insurance. Many insurance companies will not insure anyone who is over a certain weight for their height. And even those who do obtain medical insurance often find that the policy will not cover treatment for obesity because it is considered cosmetic rather than medically necessary. Advocacy groups have been trying to educate insurers about the medical risks of obesity. They have also asked the government to pass laws requiring coverage for obesity treatments. In February 2003 the estate of a deceased, morbidly obese Washington, D.C., man sued a health care insurance provider for not covering the costs of a surgical treatment for obesity that could have saved his life. The court ruled that discrimination against the man occurred on the basis of personal appearance and disability. Advocates for the rights of the obese are hailing this decision as a huge step forward in fighting such discrimination.

However, even government-funded insurance plans like Medicare and Medicaid still do not consider obesity to be a disease and will not pay for treatments related to it unless the diagnosis given is other health problems, such as heart disease or arthritis. Organizations like the American Obesity Association are trying to change this by getting the government to classify obesity as a disease. One argument they use is that obesity causes numerous medical conditions and hundreds of thousands of premature deaths each year in addition to consuming billions of dollars in related costs that could be saved by dealing with obesity itself. Another is that many other conditions, such as type 2 diabetes, cancer, and heart disease, can be affected by personal behavior other than overeating and are covered by these types of insurance, so it is discriminatory not to cover obesity on the basis that it is dependent on personal behavior rather than being a specific disease.

Although many public and private insurers will not yet cover treatments for obesity, since the year 2000, the Internal Revenue Service has allowed taxpayers to deduct the cost of weight-loss programs as a medical expense if the program is recommended by a physician to treat an existing disease such as heart disease.

Frustrations Related to Weight-Loss Failure

In addition to the financial stresses involved in trying to treat obesity by losing weight, especially frustrating for many obese people is the failure of these attempts to actually succeed. One woman, for example, joined a weight-loss program and lost thirty pounds, then gained fifty, lost the fifty pounds and gained one hundred. She became overwhelmed by depression and anxiety.

Experts say that there are many reasons for this up and down weight loss and gain. One primary reason is that the diet plan the person is following is not a good one to retain long-term healthy

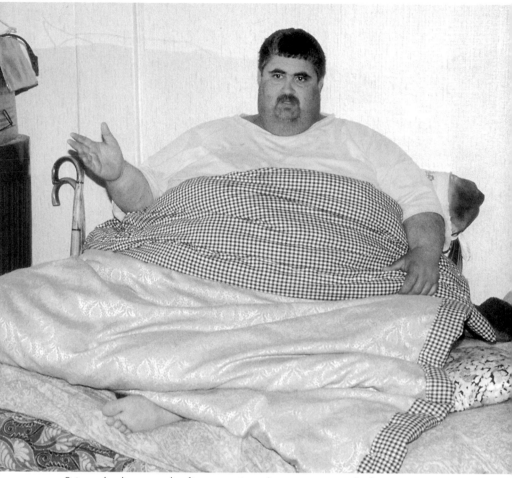

Extremely obese people often cannot receive necessary medical treatment because of their size and weight. Some have even died because they could not be properly treated.

eating habits. Another is that some people eat for comfort and abandon their program if they become stressed. One woman learned as a child that eating was a way of dealing with whatever came along. "My childhood was filled with 'eat something, you'll feel better,'"[21] she explains. She continued this behavior into adulthood, eating every time she felt anxious or angry or sad. This made it extremely difficult for her to stick with a prescribed diet plan.

This obese mother and daughter are learning how to eat a healthy diet. They are carefully monitoring both their caloric intake and the types of food they are eating.

Other times an obese individual is not really aware of how much he or she is eating. This is why it is important for the person to keep a food diary or count calories to better succeed in weight-loss efforts. Roger, for example, who weighed 340 pounds, told his doctor he was eating a modest amount of food for each meal. He did not mention that he was actually consuming a gallon of whole milk with breakfast alone. The milk did not seem important to him, nor did the tremendous amounts of food he took in seem anything but "modest" in his mind.

Whatever the reasons for an obese person having difficulty losing weight, this tendency can make them vulnerable to advertisers' proclaiming quick or miraculous weight-loss schemes. According to the American Obesity Association, many obese people are so desperate for any solution to their problem that they buy into fraudulent products and services. Such fraud often keeps them from seeking legitimate help from a physician or a worthwhile weight-loss program. Fraudulent schemes also eat up large sums of money even though they provide no benefit, and this adds to the obese person's sense of failure.

The Federal Trade Commission has filed numerous charges against providers of diet pills, potions, and devices, and warns that consumers should be careful about investing in questionable schemes. The main thing that government authorities say to keep in mind is that there are no quick and easy weight-loss solutions, so claims of that nature should be viewed with skepticism. "Any claims that you can lose weight effortlessly are false. The only proven way to lose weight is either to reduce the number of calories you eat or to increase the number of calories you burn off through exercise,"[22] points out the Food and Drug Administration.

When Weight Loss Happens

For those who find a legitimate way to lose significant amounts of weight and succeed in the endeavor, the emotional, social, and physical rewards are immense. Many people find their self-esteem improves, along with their social life and general lifestyle. No longer do they have to put up with nasty comments about their fatness. One teenaged girl who lost fifty pounds was thrilled to be able to go to the beach and wear a bathing suit without embarrassment for the first time in years. A woman who lost one hundred pounds was excited about not having to buy two seats on an airplane, because she could now fit into one. A man who went from 440 to 220 pounds said:

> My self image greatly improved. I could buy clothes in my new size almost anywhere, in a great variety of styles and colors. I could wear blue jeans and find them to fit. I went from a size 22–23 shirt, 66 inch waist pants to a man's 16–16½ shirt and 40–42 pants. I could fit comfortably in even small-size cars. I purchased a Toyota Celica, which would not have been possible earlier.[23]

A successful dieter is proud of how much weight she has lost. Obese persons who lose weight often experience improved self-esteem, greater confidence, and enhanced enjoyment of life.

Along with the social and practical improvements, weight loss also has a big impact on overall health. Blood pressure, and cholesterol and other blood fats that are often elevated in obese persons, are lowered, and many people with type 2 diabetes no longer have to take medication. Improvements in breathing and lung function are seen, and those with arthritis and other joint problems often see big improvements. Walking up a flight of stairs becomes easier; taking a hike or riding a bicycle becomes possible. Essentially, say most individuals who achieve the goal of adequate weight loss, every aspect of life from physical health to emotional well-being benefits.

Chapter 5

The Future

BECAUSE OF THE rising economic and medical burdens imposed by the explosion of worldwide obesity, lawmakers as well as health care experts are focusing on doing something to reduce the growing incidence of this condition. Major priorities for the future include developing more effective methods of preventing and treating the disorder.

The World Health Organization (WHO) has initiated public-awareness campaigns throughout the world to educate policy makers, the public, and medical professionals on the various causes of and treatments for obesity. WHO is working with the University of Sydney in Australia to calculate the worldwide economic impact of obesity, and they are collaborating with the University of Auckland in New Zealand to study the political, socioeconomic, cultural, and physical factors that promote obesity. The hope is that their research will lead to effective methods of curbing the worldwide epidemic of obesity, and they are actively trying to enlist the support of government officials everywhere to assist in this battle.

Government Efforts in the United States

In the United States, government officials are already deeply involved in trying to stem the tide of obesity. According to the Centers for Disease Control and Prevention, "One of the national health objectives for the year 2010 is to reduce the prevalence of obesity among adults to less than 15%."[24] The government has an economic interest as well as a humanitarian compunction to do something about the obesity problem. Since the federal government foots the bill for about half of the $93 billion in annual medical bills related to complications from obesity, it has determined that obesity is a social as well as a personal issue.

The Office of the Surgeon General of the United States is one of the primary government organizations involved in issuing recommendations on ways of fighting the obesity problem. Several areas are being emphasized, including the following. The surgeon general is focusing on changing peoples' perceptions of being overweight and obese so the emphasis will be on health rather than merely on appearance. This involves educating the public on what constitutes healthy eating and encouraging people to

The U.S. government helps to educate the public about healthy foods. Its guidelines include eating lots of fresh fruits and vegetables like these.

consume a healthy diet for optimal well-being. Another area of emphasis is educating expectant mothers about the benefits of breast-feeding, which seems to provide later protection against obesity in children.

To help combat obesity in children, schools are being encouraged to require physical education in all grades. Currently, only Illinois requires physical education for grades K–12 and only about 25 percent of teenagers nationwide participate in physical education. Schools are also being encouraged to provide healthier foods like fresh fruits and vegetables, whole grains, and low-fat dairy products in cafeterias. The surgeon general has recommended that, outside of school, kids get more exercise too—at least one hour most days of the week.

For adults, the recommendation for physical activity is at least thirty minutes a day. In addition, people of all ages are being encouraged to watch less television and to replace it with active pastimes. The federal government is also pushing employers and local governments to provide more opportunities for exercise at workplaces and through safe and accessible public recreation facilities.

Efforts by Lawmakers

In addition to these recommendations by the Office of the Surgeon General, lawmakers on the federal, state, and local levels are enacting legislation to help reduce the obesity problem. In New York, for example, state lawmakers have proposed a bill that requires fruit and yogurt to replace candy bars and chips in school vending machines. Other state bills under consideration would increase the number of hours of physical education required in schools and would mandate restaurants to list calories and nutritional content of the foods they serve.

In some areas, local school districts have already implemented similar requirements. Some school vending machines already offer healthier choices and some cafeterias provide more low-calorie alternatives to high-fat, high-sugar fare. In Los Angeles, schools are prohibited from selling sodas, since sodas and other sugary drinks are chock-full of calories that contribute to obesity.

The high-fat junk food found in most vending machines may soon be replaced with more healthy choices. Many school districts already offer students healthy choices such as fruit and yogurt.

Similar legislation is under consideration in the U.S. Congress as well. The Improved Nutrition and Physical Activity Act introduced in June 2003, for instance, attempts to educate the public about healthier food choices and lifestyles. It also would provide funding to train health care professionals in diagnosis and treatment of obesity. Money would also be provided for community- and school-based educational programs. Additional research into trends in fitness, obesity among different socioeconomic groups, and other topics related to the prevention and treatment of obesity would also be funded.

Other legislation is attempting to require medical insurers to pay for procedures like gastric bypass surgery for morbidly obese people for whom dieting and other measures fail.

Lawmakers in the United States may also consider legislation to add a tax on fatty foods such as cake and preprocessed meals. This type of tax is now under consideration in Australia and England for foods like chips, sweets, hamburgers, and soft drinks. Such measures are designed to discourage people from buying these foods and to repay the government for the billions of dollars it spends each year on obesity-related problems. One expert in England estimated that a fatty-food tax could prevent about a thousand premature deaths per year in that country alone. However, other experts have argued that such a tax would harm low-income families, which often eat many high-fat foods because such foods tend to be inexpensive. The debate is ongoing, and as of 2003, a fatty-food value-added tax has not been implemented.

Research on Obesity-Related Medical Problems

Along with governmental efforts to reduce obesity through legislation and education, there is a great deal of obesity-related research being conducted by government-sponsored and privately funded scientists. Some researchers are studying the relationship between obesity and various medical problems. One study at the Medical Research Council (MRC) Childhood Nutrition Research

Teen Medical Problems Associated with Obesity

- High levels of the hormone leptin

- Early signs of cardiovascular disease

- Atherosclerosis (hardening of the arteries)

- Impaired glucose tolerance

- Type 2 diabetes

Center in London, England, for example, found that teenagers with high levels of the hormone leptin had early signs of cardiovascular disease. This was indicated by a loss of elasticity in artery walls, a typical early sign of heart disease. The researchers found the same phenomenon in laboratory animals and believe the high levels of leptin may help explain how obesity is linked to atherosclerosis, the thickening and stiffening of the arteries that often goes along with cardiovascular disease. The researchers explain that "Our study suggests a way in which obesity decreases the elasticity of blood vessels, thus increasing the risk of heart disease. Preventing even moderate fatness in childhood may have a long-term benefit for the risk of heart disease."[25] Further studies to determine how leptin impairs arteries and to find out whether reducing leptin levels decreases cardiovascular disease are planned.

Other research on preventing the complications of obesity includes a study funded by the National Institutes of Health. This study, released in March 2003, found that many obese children and adolescents have impaired glucose tolerance, a condition that appears before the individual develops type 2 diabetes. Experts say this knowledge may provide a way of preventing type 2 diabetes in those children and teens who have impaired glucose tolerance and are able to lose weight. Type 2 diabetes is a disease that afflicted virtually no children or teens prior to the 1990s. Now, with the increase in obesity in these age groups, it has become increasingly prevalent.

Another medical problem linked to obesity is birth defects. A study conducted during the 1990s, by the Centers for Disease Control and Prevention, found that obese women are more likely to have a baby with spina bifida, omphalocele, heart defects, and multiple anomalies. Spina bifida results from the failure of the spine to close properly. The newborn may require surgery to repair the defect and the complications it causes. Individuals with spina bifida generally suffer many physical and mental handicaps. Omphalocele is a defect where some of the abdominal organs protrude from the base of the umbilical cord. It requires surgery to repair. Oftentimes other birth defects go along with this condition. The researchers emphasize that the study shows the importance of obese women losing weight before becoming pregnant.

Genetic Research into the Causes of Obesity

Investigations into the causes of obesity are another area of intense research. Some studies are looking at the role of certain genes in causing obesity. In one project, researchers at the University of California, Los Angeles, at Merck & Company, and at Rosetta Inpharmatics found many obesity-related genes on chromosome number two in mice. They also found that different genes contribute to two different breeds of overweight mice. They hope that treatments that target specific genes can be developed for each group. They also hope to determine similar genetic patterns and targeted treatments in humans.

Genetic research by Dr. Salih Wakil and his colleagues at Baylor College of Medicine in Houston, Texas, has discovered that mice genetically engineered to lack an enzyme called acetyl-CoA carboxylase2 (ACC2) are able to eat 20–30 percent more food while accumulating less fat and weighing about 10 percent less than normal mice. The investigators found that these mice burn more fat than normal mice do. According to an article published by the National Institute of General Medical Sciences, "If Dr. Wakil's results in mice hold true for humans, then a drug that blocks the function of ACC2 might allow people to lose weight while maintaining a normal diet."[26]

Another group of investigators at the National Institutes of Health in Bethesda, Maryland, found that children with a mutation in a gene that produces an enzyme known as 11betaHSD-1 are more likely to be overweight or obese than other kids. The enzyme converts cortisone, a naturally occurring steroid, into cortisol. An excess of cortisol is linked to central obesity, which is the type of obesity where fat accumulates around the waist. Central obesity has been linked to a tendency to develop insulin resistance, diabetes, and heart disease. The researchers hope their work will eventually lead to treatment with drugs targeting the gene mutation.

Other Research into the Causes of Obesity

Besides the research on genetic causes of obesity, scientists are also looking at other factors that contribute to the development of the disorder. Dr. Allan Levine at the Veterans Affairs Medical Center in Minneapolis, Minnesota, for example, is investigating the role of brain chemistry in obesity and overeating. Levine found that endorphins, brain chemicals similar to the narcotic opium, are one of the chemicals that initiate a feeling of pleasure after people eat sweet foods. He is looking for brain chemicals or parts of the brain that are involved in cravings for sweets in hopes of developing drugs that will dampen this craving.

So far, Levine has discovered that a part of the brain stimulated by sugar is the same part stimulated by addictive drugs. This could be why sugar intake is important in obesity. Research shows that many obese people crave sweets, and investigators believe this may be because these people have a defect in the way the brain processes certain brain chemicals. As explained in a recent article:

> Researchers have found that eating carbohydrates [sugars] raises levels of the amino acid tryptophan in the bloodstream. The brain converts tryptophan into serotonin. Serotonin is a brain chemical regulating mood and sleepiness. Carbohydrate cravers are thought to have a faulty serotonin feedback mechanism. As a result, their bodies never stop craving carbohydrates.[27]

Related research at the National Institute on Drug Abuse sheds further light on how brain chemistry may underlie obesity. The study found that obese individuals share certain abnormal brain characteristics with drug addicts. Such individuals have abnormally few nerve cell components known as D2 receptors, which pick up the neurotransmitter dopamine in the brain; dopamine contributes to feelings of pleasure.

Researchers believe that people with a deficiency of D2 receptors do not receive normal feelings of pleasure after activities like eating. Therefore, they may need to overeat to get feelings of gratification from food. A similar deficiency has been proven to

Studies show that sugary foods trigger a release of chemicals in the brain that initiate a feeling of pleasure. As a result, sugar can cause a craving that is difficult to resist.

underlie drug addictions. Thus, researchers suggest, a deficiency of D2 receptors may be linked to a variety of compulsive behaviors. One investigator explains: "Although many complex factors may be involved in excessive behaviors such as compulsive drug abuse, overeating, and gambling, they are all similar in that the brain is changed, reward circuits are disrupted, and the behavior eventually becomes involuntary."[28]

Does a Virus Cause Obesity?

One other line of research is exploring whether a virus may be responsible for some cases of obesity. Nikhil Dhurandhar and Richard L. Atkinson at the University of Wisconsin in Madison have discovered that a virus known as Ad-36 may influence obesity. Ad-36 produces cold symptoms and is related to the SMAM-1 virus, which Dhurandhar originally studied in India. There he found that chickens killed by this virus had large amounts of body fat. Wondering if this virus was related to obesity in humans, Dhurandhar found that a group of patients who showed antibodies to SMAM-1 in their blood (which indicated they had been infected by the virus) were also heavier than normal.

When the U.S. Department of Agriculture would not allow the researchers to import the SMAM-1 virus into the United States, the researchers found a similar virus, Ad-36, already present in this country. They found that chickens infected with the Ad-36 virus had higher body fat content than other chickens, even though they did not eat more. The same was found to be true in mice, marmosets, and monkeys. The researchers then tested humans for antibodies to Ad-36, since they could not ethically infect people with the virus. These antibodies would be evidence of a previous infection with the Ad-36 virus. They found that 15 percent of obese people in the study had such antibodies. None of the lean people had them. Later studies showed that 32 percent of obese test subjects had antibodies to Ad-36.

The researchers are uncertain of how this virus might cause obesity, but believe it may have something to do with the fact that animals exposed to Ad-36 have more and larger fat cells. Many other scientists are skeptical about the theory that a virus is even related to obesity, and further research is planned to determine whether the Ad-36 virus or other viruses are actually a contributing cause.

Drug Research

In addition to the studies being conducted on the causes of obesity, there is a great deal of research on new drug treatments for the disorder. New drugs are originally tested on animals in a laboratory. Once a compound has been proven to be safe and effective in a laboratory setting, the drug developer may apply to the U.S. Food and Drug Administration or to comparable agencies in other countries to begin testing on humans in clinical trials.

After a drug has successfully completed clinical trials, doctors can begin prescribing the new compound for people not included in the trials. Sometimes, however, problems with a drug do not show up until after it has been on the market for some time. This is what happened with the dangerous diet drug fen-phen, which caused heart damage and many deaths and was subsequently removed from the market in 1997.

New Drugs Being Tested

There are hundreds of drugs in various stages of clinical trials being tested for treatment of obesity. Some, like Amylin, work by enhancing the effects of insulin. This allows the body to more efficiently metabolize food and to release a satiety factor that acts to suppress the appetite after eating. This decreases food intake and leads to weight loss. Others, like botanical P57, made from a South African cactus, suppress the appetite while reducing the amount of fat in the liver. Aminosterol, also known as MSI-1436, is another type of appetite suppressant being tested. It comes from the dogfish shark and has been proven to suppress the appetite in laboratory mice, rats, dogs, and monkeys and appears to be safe, but human testing remains to be done. Scientists speculate that the presence of MSI-1436 in dogfish sharks produces this fish's odd behavior of eating only once every two weeks. They believe the chemical works by altering calcium signals in the brain.

The side effects of certain weight-loss drugs are not revealed in laboratory tests. This woman claims that fen-phen, which she took while pregnant, caused her son's birth defects.

Cholecystokinin-A (CCK-A) promoters are a class of drugs that work by slowing down the rate at which the stomach empties, thereby making someone feel full longer. There are several of these CCK-A promoters being tested for the treatment of obesity. One is Satietrol, which prolongs the time that CCK-A stays in the stomach. This slows down the rate at which the stomach empties by prolonging satiety signals sent to the brain. Doctors are hopeful that this drug will result in less food being eaten.

Human growth hormone fragment is another drug being developed and tested. Human growth hormone, which normally decreases with age, cannot be used as a weight-loss treatment because of numerous adverse effects, including insulin resistance, high blood pressure, and dangerous changes in bones and muscles. However, scientists have isolated a small region of the growth hormone molecule that dissolves fat but has none of the adverse effects attributed to the complete molecule. Investigators are exploring the use of this human growth hormone fragment as a weight-loss drug.

Health and Human Services secretary Tommy Thompson (right) believes that obesity is one of the most pressing new health challenges of today.

Other Research on Drugs

Besides developing and testing new drugs for the treatment of obesity, there is also research directed at understanding exactly how existing drugs work. Research on the appetite suppressant drug D-fenfluramine, for example, showed that the drug increases the release of the neurotransmitter serotonin in the brain. Serotonin is a chemical that curbs appetite by affecting nerve cells known as melanocortin neurons in the arcuate nucleus region of the hypothalamus, an area of the brain correlated with appetite and energy expenditure. Serotonin affects these neurons by causing them to fire twice as fast as normal. This in turn has the effect of suppressing the appetite. "Our study has linked the serotonin system, a classic brain pathway thought to be involved with eating disorders like anorexia nervosa, to the melanocortin system, a brain pathway involved in obesity,"[29] explains the study's senior author, neuroscientist Joel Elmquist. The researchers hope their project will help doctors better understand the causes of obesity as well as lead to the development of newer, better drugs that suppress the appetite in a similar manner.

Other Research on Prevention and Treatment

Besides the many studies on treating obesity with drugs, there is a great deal of research being conducted on the role of exercise and diet in preventing and treating obesity. One study at the University of Minnesota in Minneapolis, for example, assessed whether strength-training exercises performed twice weekly could help prevent fat gain in middle-aged women. The researchers found that, while such exercise did not lead to weight loss, it did produce an increase in fat-free mass and a decrease in body-fat content. They are hopeful that their research will lead people to perform this type of exercise in an effort to enhance fat loss and prevent age-related weight gain.

Research into the efficacy of certain diets in weight-loss efforts includes a study on the safety and effectiveness of low-carbohydrate diets. The study concluded that there is not enough scientific evidence to say whether or not these diets work better than other reduced-calorie diets in helping people to lose weight. More research on the subject is planned to assess whether or not people who follow such diets are actually achieving safe and optimal weight-reduction results.

Goals for the Future

The goal of all of this research into causes, treatments, and control of obesity is, of course, to help reduce the incidence of this disorder. Public officials and medical experts are hoping that these efforts yield positive results in the very near future, since rising rates of obesity have made fighting the trend a high public health priority. In the words of U.S. Health and Human Services secretary Tommy Thompson,

> Overweight and obesity are among the most pressing new health challenges we face today. Our modern environment has allowed these conditions to increase at alarming rates and become a growing health problem for our nation. By confronting these conditions, we have tremendous opportunities to prevent the unnecessary disease and disability they portend for our future.[30]

Notes

Introduction: A Growing Health Problem
1. World Health Organization, "Controlling the Global Obesity Epidemic." www.who.int.

Chapter 1: What Is Obesity?
2. American Obesity Association, "What Is Obesity?" www.obesity.org.
3. American Obesity Association, "Obesity Is a Chronic Disease." www.obesity.org.
4. Centers for Disease Control and Prevention, "Obesity and Genetics." www.cdc.gov.

Chapter 2: What Causes Obesity?
5. Norman B. Ackerman, *Fat No More,* Amherst, NY: Prometheus Books, 1999, p. 33.
6. Centers for Disease Control and Prevention, "Obesity and Genetics: What We Know, What We Don't Know and What It Means." www.cdc.gov.
7. American Obesity Association, "Obesity—A Global Epidemic." www.obesity.org.
8. Mark Abramovitz, interview with the author, San Luis Obispo, CA, September 2003.
9. American Obesity Association, "My Story." www.obesity.org.

Chapter 3: How Is Obesity Treated?
10. National Heart, Lung, and Blood Institute, "Selecting a Weight Loss Program." www.nhlbi.nih.gov.
11. U.S. Food and Drug Administration, "The Facts About Weight Loss Products and Programs." http://vm.cfsan.fda.gov.

12. Ackerman, *Fat No More*, p. 47.
13. Abraham C. Kuruwilla, "Acupuncture and Obesity," American Academy of Medical Acupuncture. www.medical acupuncture.org.

Chapter 4: Living with Obesity

14. American Obesity Association, "My Story."
15. American Obesity Association, "My Story."
16. American Obesity Association, "My Story."
17. American Obesity Association, "My Story."
18. David Brown, "Study Cites Pervasive Effects of Obesity in Children," *Washington Post*, April 9, 2003, p. A10.
19. Quoted in Ackerman, *Fat No More*, p. 204.
20. J. Eric Oliver and Taeku Lee, "Public Opinion and the Politics of America's Obesity Epidemic," Social Science Research Network (SSRN) Electronic Library. http://papers.ssrn.com.
21. American Obesity Association, "My Story."
22. U.S. Food and Drug Administration, "The Facts about Weight Loss Products and Programs."
23. Quoted in Ackerman, *Fat No More*, p. 200.

Chapter 5: The Future

24. Centers for Disease Control and Prevention, "Overweight and Obesity." www.cdc.gov.
25. Quoted in American Heart Association, "Elevated Leptin in Teens Linked with Dangerous Artery Changes." www.americanheart.org.
26. Alisa Zapp Machalek, "Designer Mice Eat More, Weigh Less," National Institute of General Medical Sciences. www.nigms.nih.gov.
27. Rob Schmitz, "Obesity and the Brain," Minnesota Public Radio: News. http://news.mpr.org.
28. Robert Mathias, "Pathological Obesity and Drug Addiction Share Common Brain Characteristics," *NIDA Notes*, October 2001. www.drugabuse.gov.
29. Quoted in National Institutes of Health, "Drug Targets Brain Circuits That Drive Appetite and Body Weight," News Release, July 25, 2002. www.nih.gov.

30. Quoted in U.S. Department of Health and Human Services, "Overweight and Obesity Threaten U.S. Health Gains," December 13, 2001. www.surgeongeneral.gov.

Glossary

anthropometry: Methods of measuring body fat.

bariatric surgery: Surgery to treat morbid obesity.

body mass index: A commonly used measurement of body weight relative to height used to calculate whether someone is overweight or obese.

calorie: A measure of heat used in dietetics for measuring the heat content of a food, or the amount of energy it can yield as it passes through the body.

carbohydrate: A major source of energy in the diet. There are two types of carbohydrates—simple sugars and complex carbohydrates.

chromosomes: Wormlike bodies in the center of each cell where genes reside.

diet: Any type of eating plan.

genes: The part of a DNA molecule that passes hereditary information from parents to their offspring.

ileum: The lower small intestine.

jejunum: The upper small intestine.

morbid obesity: A condition in which being overweight is likely to bring about major medical problems.

obesity: Having more body fat as a percentage of body weight than normal.

overweight: Too much body weight relative to height.

Organizations to Contact

American Obesity Association
1250 24th St. NW, Suite 300
Washington, DC, 20037
(202) 776-7711
www.obesity.org

The American Obesity Association offers comprehensive information and advocacy for obese persons.

Office of the Surgeon General of the United States
5600 Fishers Ln., Room 18-66
Rockville, MD 20857
www.surgeongeneral.gov

The surgeon general's office provides fact sheets and press releases on all aspects of obesity and its related complications.

The National Heart, Lung, and Blood Institute
NHLBI Health Information Center
PO Box 30105
Bethesda, MD 20824-0105
(301) 592-8573
www.nhlbi.nih.gov

The NHLBI offers a series of practical articles on weight reduction and healthy eating.

North American Association for the Study of Obesity
8630 Fenton St., Suite 918
Silver Spring, MD 20910

(301) 563-6526

www.naaso.org

The NAASO is a scientific society dedicated to studying obesity. The website offers comprehensive information on all aspects of obesity.

WIN, the Weight Control Information Network of the National Institute of Diabetes & Digestive & Kidney Diseases (NIDDK)
1 Win Way
Bethesda, MD 20892-3665
(877) 946-4627
www.niddk.nih.gov

A part of the National Institutes of Health, WIN provides information on weight control and nutrition.

For Further Reading

Books

Dana K. Cassell and Donald H. Gleaves, *Encyclopedia of Obesity and Eating Disorders*. New York: Facts On File, 2000. Four hundred alphabetized entries explaining all aspects of obesity and other eating disorders.

J. Clinton Smith, *Understanding Childhood Obesity*. Jackson: University Press of Mississippi, 1999. Covers research, causes, prevention, and treatments related to obesity in children.

Melinda S. Southern, T. Kristian von Almen, and Heidi Schumacher, *Trim Kids*. New York: Harper Resource, 2001. A weight-loss plan to help kids develop healthy, lifelong eating habits.

Internet Sources

Child Trends DataBank, "Overweight Children and Youth." www.childtrendsdatabank.org.

4 Girls Health, "You Are What You Eat." www.4girls.gov.

Works Consulted

Books

Norman B. Ackerman, *Fat No More*. Amherst, NY: Prometheus Books, 1999. Easily understood explanation of obesity and surgical treatments for the condition.

Kelly D. Brownell and Christopher G. Fairburn, eds., *Eating Disorders and Obesity*. New York: Guilford Press, 1995. Comprehensive technical articles on all aspects of obesity.

Periodicals

David Brown, "Study Cites Pervasive Effects of Obesity in Children," *Washington Post*, April 9, 2003.

Business Wire, "Regeneron Announces Results of Phase III Obesity Study," March 31, 2003.

Tom Corwin, "Doctors Tie Obesity to Genes, Culture," *Augusta Chronicle*, February 6, 2003.

Philippe Froguel and Philippe Boutin, "Genetics of Pathways Regulating Body Weight in the Development of Obesity in Humans," *Experimental Biology and Medicine*, December 2001.

Guy Gugliotta, "Heart Association Urges Federal Ban on Ephedra," *Washington Post*, April 4, 2003.

Nanci Hellmich, "An Overweight America Comes with a Hefty Price Tag," *USA Today*, May 14, 2003.

K.H. Schmitz, et al., "Strength Training for Obesity Prevention in Midlife Women," *International Journal of Obesity Related Metabolic Disorders*, March 2003.

Shawna Vogel, "Why We Get Fat," *Discover*, April 1999.

Margaret L. Watkins, et al., "Maternal Obesity and Risk for Birth Defects," *Pediatrics*, May 2003.

Internet Sources

American Heart Association, "Elevated Leptin in Teens Linked with Dangerous Artery Changes." www.americanheart.org.

American Obesity Association, "Causes of Obesity." www.obesity.org.

——, "Court Upholds Discrimination Claim Against Insurance Companies Brought by Estate of Morbidly Obese Man."

——, "My Story."

——, "Obesity—A Global Epidemic."

——, "Obesity Is a Chronic Disease."

——, "What Is Obesity?"

American Society for Bariatric Surgery, "Rationale for the Surgical Treatment of Morbid Obesity." www.asbs.org.

BBC News, "Obesity Gene Pinpointed." http://news.bbc.co.uk.

Centers for Disease Control and Prevention, "Obesity and Genetics." www.cdc.gov.

——, "Obesity and Genetics: What We Know, What We Don't Know and What It Means."

——, "Overweight and Obesity."

Abraham C. Kuruwilla, "Acupuncture and Obesity," American Academy of Medical Acupuncture. www.medicalacupuncture.org.

Alisa Zapp Machalek, "Designer Mice Eat More, Weigh Less," National Institute of General Medical Sciences. www.nigms.nih.gov.

Liza Jane Maltin, "Insulin Pill Fights Obesity," WebMD Medical News, MSN Health. http://content.health.msn.com.

Robert Mathias, "Pathological Obesity and Drug Addiction Share Common Brain Characteristics," National Institute on Drug Abuse, *NIDA Notes*, October 2001. www.drugabuse.com.

National Heart, Lung, and Blood Institute, "Selecting a Weight Loss Program." www.nhlbi.nih.gov.

National Institutes of Health, "Drug Targets Brain Circuits That Drive Appetite and Body Weight," News Release, July 25, 2002. www.nih.gov.

Office of the Surgeon General, "Overweight and Obesity: A Vision for The Future." www.surgeongeneral.gov.

J. Eric Oliver and Taeku Lee, "Public Opinion and the Politics of America's Obesity Epidemic," Social Science Research Network (SSRN) Electronic Library. http://papers.ssrn.com.

Andrea Orr, "CDC: Obesity, Fastest Growing Health Threat in U.S.," Reuters Foundation, AlertNet. www.alertnet.org.

Reuters Health, "Gene Mutation May Play a Role in Childhood Obesity." www.nlm.nih.gov.

Rockefeller University, "Obesity Not a Personal Failing, Says Leptin Discoverer Jeffrey Friedman, but a Battle Against Biology." www.rockefeller.edu.

Rob Schmitz, "Obesity and the Brain," Minnesota Public Radio: News. http://news.mpr.org.

U.S. Department of Health and Human Services, "Overweight and Obesity Threaten U.S. Health Gains," December 13, 2001. www.surgeongeneral.gov.

U.S. Food and Drug Administration, "The Facts About Weight Loss Products and Programs." http://vm.cfsan.fda.gov.

Lidia Wasowicz, "Obesity Found to Have Many Varied Causes," United Press International. www.upi.com.

World Health Organization, "Controlling the Global Obesity Epidemic." www.who.int.

Index

Picture Credits

Cover Photo: © Mauro Fermariello/SPL/Photo Researchers
© ABC Basin Ajansi/CORBIS SYGMA, 73
© Paul Almasy/CORBIS, 20,
© AP/Wide World Photos, 57, 89
© Bettmann/CORBIS, 22, 35, 50, 70
© Corel, 54, 86
© Mitchell Gerber/CORBIS, 32
© David M. Grossman/Phototake, 26
© John Henley/CORBIS, 62
© Hulton/Archive by Getty Images, 12, 38
© Dan Lamont/CORBIS, 14
© Landov, 90
© Erich Lessing/ Art Resource, NY, 11
© Roy Morsch/CORBIS, 28
© Photodisc, 25, 31, 40, 43, 47, 51, 55, 60, 79
© Mark Richards/CORBIS, 66, 74
© Scott Sommerdorf/San Francisco Chronicle/CORBIS, 69
© Russell Underwood/CORBIS, 81
© Forestier Yves/CORBIS SYGMA, 76

About the Author

Melissa Abramovitz grew up in San Diego, California, and developed an interest in medical topics as a teenager. She began college with the intention of becoming a doctor, but later switched majors and graduated summa cum laude from the University of California, San Diego, with a degree in psychology in 1976.

She launched her career as a writer in 1986 to allow her to be an at-home mom when her two children were small, realized she had found her niche, and continues to freelance regularly for a variety of magazines and educational book publishers. In her seventeen years as a freelance writer, she has published hundreds of nonfiction articles and numerous short stories, poems, and books for children, teenagers, and adults. Many of her works are on medical topics.

At the present time, she lives in San Luis Obispo, California, with her husband and two college-age sons.